The Woodworking Bible

A Step-by-Step Guide to Crafting Wood Dreams on a Budget – Tools, Techniques, and Amazing DIY Projects You Can Be Proud of, even if You're Time-Pressed or an Absolute Beginner

Bruce Merrick

Reading Roads Press

A Publishing Company

EXTRA CONTENT

Join us on an exclusive journey!

Uncover a treasure trove of extra content and additional resources waiting for you to explore and enjoy.

Scan the QR-code or follow the link below to access everything:

http://www.readingroadspress.com/woodworking-bonus

Table of Contents

Introduction

Deciding to be a woodworker is a brilliant move. It's enjoyable, soothing, gratifying, and even very productive! But for beginners, woodworking is often the opposite of all these things, as it requires a certain level of knowledge before you start crafting your first successful projects. This book will cover the basics of what you need to make sure you get started the right way and enjoy the process.

You need to be educated first.

Secondly, you need to have the right tools, but let's not go crazy with this step now. There is a limited set of essential tools that should be owned by every woodworker, including mallets, chisels, a hand plane, clamps, wood glue, a quality bits drill, tape measure, wood square, carpenter pencils, hammer, nails, and sandpaper. Initially, purchase those; then, as you start working on different projects, buy the tools required for each specific design. You will eventually have quite an impressive workshop. But take it slowly, and always be sure to buy high-quality tools. When it comes to woodworking equipment, seek quality over quantity.

You'll need good plans, at last.

The most important point to remember about beginners' woodworking, when it's all said and done, is to take it slow. Work on improving any new ability when your path comes. Above all, focus on your new skill and personalize it. Afterward, move on to the next skill and strive to master it once again. Then, focus on building your toolbox and other necessary resources as you aim for higher levels of expertise.

Whether you're interested in creating an odd piece of furniture you can proudly claim as your own, or saving money by repairing and refurbishing the wooden furniture that's wearing and tearing around your home, or even launching your woodworking business, you've come to the right place!

Undoubtedly, to learn this craft, having an experienced woodworker by your side is invaluable. However, many people may not seek guidance from experts, as they pursue woodworking as a hobby rather than a professional endeavor.

You must understand that woodworking can be a hard job, particularly when undertaken without proper guidance. This is precisely why this book exists. Within its pages, you will uncover a treasure trove of invaluable insights and knowledge tailored for beginners. With dedication and adherence to these guidelines, you'll not only accelerate your learning curve but also transform your woodworking endeavors into masterpieces of fine craftsmanship.

Simple tips to prepare you to become a better woodworker

- **Start Small.** When you're just starting, you might be tempted to go out and splurge on all the best woodworking equipment you can buy. Several hardware stores profit from this increased interest in woodworking by selling you expensive equipment you don't need right now. Yes, it's essential to have the right woodworking tools, but you can start with only the basics while learning the craft. Simple, inexpensive tools are more than enough to get you started on small projects such as a birdhouse or a small coffee table. It helps you get a sense of woodworking and builds confidence for more complex projects. Begin from the ground always with learning the basics. You can learn about, for example, the different forms of woodworking, the types of trees and wood that you can use, the tools for the work, etc.

- **Do good research.** Once you've decided on a project, don't assume you know how to build it immediately. The very essence of enjoyable woodworking is careful planning and preparation. It is even more necessary for beginners to double and triple check the design and quantity bill before starting work because a lack of preparation can lead to hours of frustration and waste of valuable materials. Know precisely what tools and materials you need for your project, and how much energy and time you need to put in to get your project done. For easy reference, ensure you print a hard copy of your bill of quantities while you're shopping for materials, and a hard copy of your convenience plans while working on your project.

- **Always have a practical plan.** Woodworking is just like building a house. If you're serious about making woodwork of exceptional quality, get a detailed plan so you can follow it through and get the project done without wasting time.

- **Lay down your expectations.** Each project needs money. Many big projects are extremely expensive, while some cost only a little. Know how much you will need before you start your design, so you can plan for the budget you need.

- **Be consistent.** Many woodworking enthusiasts begin with enthusiasm, only to become discouraged when they fail to create the perfect version of their initial projects. Woodworking, especially for beginners, requires time to become familiar with the materials and learn how to maximize their potential. For example, some wood types are best suited for outdoor furniture, while others are better for indoor furniture. Also, some recommendations on wood that might be ideal for certain climates may not be the best for you. The creation of a good piece of woodwork takes experience and practice, so don't be discouraged if you get it wrong on the first attempt!

Chapter 1: Types of woods

There are many different species of wood that can be used for woodworking, but they can be broken into 3 primary types: softwood, hardwood, and engineered wood. This chapter introduces you to these different wood types and teaches you how to differentiate between them, which is an important skill for any woodworker, as it helps you to determine the best kind of wood for your specific project.

Hardwood vs Softwood

Hardwoods and softwoods are harvested from different types of trees: softwoods come from coniferous trees, which use needles and cones for reproduction, while hardwoods are harvested from deciduous trees, that can be found in more temperate regions, and produce seeds instead of cones. As their names suggest, hardwoods are harder than softwoods, however, it's important to note that not all hardwoods possess the same level of hardness, and the same holds true for softwoods—they do not universally share the same degree of softness. Nevertheless, as a general rule, hardwoods tend to be more challenging to work with compared to softwoods.

Hardwoods are not as sustainable as softwood trees because they take longer to grow before they are ready to be harvested. However, hardwood timber is higher in quality and more durable: as a consequence, even if this wood is quite expensive, the durability often makes it worth spending the extra money. It is usually preferred for furniture because it comes in different colors and finishes and is easy to clean and maintain. It can also be used for purposes such as flooring, paneling, cladding, building, fencing, etc. The durability of hardwood also makes it appropriate for building boats and ship decks. Some of the best-known hardwoods include mahogany, blackbutt, balsa, and eucalyptus.

Unlike hardwoods, which come from deciduous angiosperm trees, softwoods tend to come from coniferous gymnosperm trees, which are often, although not always, found in mountainous regions. These trees grow faster and are highly renewable. As the name implies, softwoods are typically weaker and softer (because softwood trees are less "dense" than the others); however, there are some hard softwoods, like juniper and yew, that are durable enough to create quality furniture. In any case, softwood is ideal for crafting lighter furniture that is easier to move. It also serves well in creating feature walls, ceilings, doors, and windows.

In general, items created with softwood can be difficult to maintain and require additional cleaning and maintenance to ensure their durability. On the other hand, softwoods are quite cheap, so they are easier to source and start working with. However, when choosing the type of timber you're going to work with, you should choose based on your purpose and the features you need: if you're planning to make something that is heavy and durable, it is best to go for hardwood, while if you're more interested in style and appearance than durability, than softwood might be better. Moreover, although softwoods are cheaper, the overall cost of making and maintaining softwood furniture could be higher because you have, for example, refinishing costs. Finally, consider that hardwoods tend to be better for indoor elements because they are more fire resistant, while softwood is appropriate for outdoor projects like doors and windows.

Types of Softwood

Cedar, pine, redwood, and fir are some of the most popular types of softwood. Thus, we'll focus on these here below.

Cedar

The most popular type of cedar is Western Red Cedar, known for its reddish hue and its status as one of the softest woods used in woodworking. It boasts a straight grain and emits a distinct aromatic scent—some carpenters believe this aroma helps protect furniture from moths and insects. Western Red Cedar is readily available in many home furniture stores, often used in crafting chests and storage closets designed to ward off pests. It is an excellent choice for outdoor furniture, making it suitable for patio furniture and decks. However, it's important to note that cedar is not suitable for kitchen furniture, bedroom furniture, or utensils, as its aromatic oils can be irritating to human skin upon contact.

Pine

Pine is another common softwood that is used in many simple projects because it is durable and affordable, making it especially appealing for amateur wood workers. It is native to various regions of the Northern Hemisphere, including North America, Europe, and Asia; due to its widespread distribution and the fact that it grows very quickly, it can be considered a sustainable resource for woodworkers.

Pine wood is usually characterized by a pale yellow to light reddish-brown heartwood, while the sapwood is nearly white. The color can vary depending on the pine species. Typically it has a straight grain with a medium to coarse texture.

Wood workers may prefer white pine or yellow pine for carving work. Unless it is properly treated to increase durability, pine should only be used to create indoor furniture and fixtures. Pine can be painted, treated, and stained to obtain different effects.

Redwood

Redwood is a softwood with a fairly reddish tint that gives completed furniture excellent color and finish. It is a truly majestic tree that in some cases (think for example of Coast Redwoods) can reach incredible heights, with some exceeding 350 feet (107 meters); it belongs to the Cupressaceae family and is native to the west coast of North America, primarily California and Oregon. Redwoods have thick, fibrous, and reddish-brown bark that acts as a natural fire-resistant shield, protecting the tree from wildfires. They grow fast and can be sourced easily from different stores, they have a straight grain and are moisture resistant, so they don't easily spoil, which makes them appropriate for creating outdoor fences, walls, and garden furniture. It is also an excellent wood for indoor furniture such as cabinets and chests.

Fir

Fir is another softwood with a reddish tint. It is firmer and harder than other softwoods, but it is also easy to source. It is good for creating a variety of furniture, but does not have an attractive grain pattern, so it is best to use it for furniture that you plan to paint.

Spruce

Spruce is a conifer softwood that comes in a light color with a subtle grain. It is not weather or moisture resistant, so it is best for indoor furniture. If allowed to grow to peak maturity, spruce has great acoustic properties, which make it particularly valuable for creating musical instruments such as guitars, pianos, and violins.

Types of Hardwood

There are different types of hardwoods available in the woodwork stores that can be used to make sturdy furniture and good indoor as well as outdoor projects. Because hardwoods take a long time to grow to maturity (and maturity is required to obtain the sturdiness they're known for), they are more expensive than softwoods. However, the money you put into good quality hardwood is worth it if you want sturdy, long-lasting furniture. There is a variety of hardwoods that match different budgets and requirements. We'll cover the most common here.

Mahogany

Mahogany is a beautiful and popular hardwood. Despite being a hardwood, it is quite soft and is easy to work with, in fact it is renowned for its workability: it can be cut, planed, and sanded smoothly, making it a joy to work with for woodworkers. It is also known for its stability and resistance to warping; moreover, it takes finishes, stains, and polishes exceptionally well, resulting in a lustrous, glossy appearance. It is reddish-brown color with a great texture and finish and is often used to create indoor fine furniture such as tables, chairs, cabinets, and decorative pieces. Because of the excellent acoustic quality of mature mahogany, it is also used to create musical instruments. Since it takes a long time to grow to maturity, its price is very high and it could be quite difficult to find in stores; this fact increases the value of any furniture created from this wood.

Cherry

Cherry is a type of hardwood that is whitish in sapwood (young cherry) and reddish brown in heartwood (mature cherry). It is easier to access and buy than mahogany, but like mahogany it is easy to work with and has a beautiful finish. Cherry typically has a straight, fine, and uniform grain pattern, often interspersed with natural mineral streaks, gum spots, and occasional irregularities; moreover it has a smooth, fine texture, making it ideal for carving, turning, and finishing, and it is dimensionally stable, meaning it resists warping and shrinking. It can be used to create tables, chairs, cabinets, dressers (its warm, reddish-brown color and elegant grain patterns add sophistication to furniture designs). Cherry's workability makes it a good choice for crafting small boxes, jewelry boxes, and other fine boxes, too. It is often used also for woodturning projects, such as bowls, vases, and decorative items, due to its smooth texture and attractive grain.

Oak

Oak is a good multi-purpose hardwood. It is harder in texture and density than mahogany and cherry, which means that it is also more difficult to work with. However, oak is preferred by woodworkers for its color and texture: it can be red or white, and both types are used to create furniture. Red oak is softer and more difficult to source, while white oak is harder and very easy to source from home furniture stores. It is a versatile wood because it can be treated and sealed to increase its moisture and rot resistance; moreover, it can be crafted to last for decades or even centuries, so rest assured that wood furniture made from oak will last for many generations.

Maple

Maple is another promising hardwood due to its beautiful color and texture. There are soft and hard maples: soft maple is preferred by wood workers because it is easier to craft with wood working tools; hard maple is difficult to work with and difficult to source. Its fine, straight grain is very stable and durable. Moreover, maple is suitable for different budgets because it is inexpensive.

Poplar

Poplar is a type of hardwood that many woodworkers prefer because it is very easy to shape and cut despite being a hardwood. Therefore, it is often used to create new furniture. The color is a dull white that is best painted to hide the texture. As said, it has great workability, but you should be careful about the tools you use, in fact blunt tools and excessive force can tear apart the wood. You should always work slowly and carefully with this wood!

Birch

Birch is a type of hardwood known for its stability and durability. Birch is available in both yellow and white varieties, while the inner heartwood of the birch has a reddish-brown tint. Birch is easy to craft and is not as expensive as other hardwoods. The wood is easy to work with, but a concern for wood workers is that it can get blotchy. Therefore, birch is good for furniture that is going to be painted and polished.

Engineered Woods

Engineered wood is the same as any other natural wood, but it is manufactured. It includes different types of hardwoods and softwoods that are mixed with additives and adhesives to create stronger wood types, so that you can access the properties of excellent natural wood that are more difficult to find. Moreover it is very sustainable because it is created from waste wood that would have otherwise been discarded. In addition, the manufacturing process removes defects and texture issues that you might encounter with natural wood by adding other chemicals that reinforce and introduce new characteristics into the pieces.

For all of these reasons, engineered woods are often a great choice for modern wood work.

However, they are not perfect: for example, since they are a composite of different woods, their texture and color might not be very appealing, and some types are also quite expensive.

Here are the most common types of engineered wood.

Plywood

Plywood is manufactured from thin layers of wood veneer that are glued together. It is created by binding resin and wood fiber sheets to form a composite material with a characteristic cross grain. Plywood has dimensional stability, but it still contracts and expands with use, so you need to put gaps in structures that incorporate plywood.

Different types of grading are used with plywood. For example, type A plywood has a smooth veneer surface that is free from knots and repairs. Type B plywood is largely free from knots, but tight knots under 1 inch that are acceptable. Type C plywood has knots that are 1.5 inch in length and knot holes that are less than 1 inch. Type D plywood has knots and knot holes up to 2.5 inches. Finally, type X plywood is created only for outdoor use and is not of the same quality as A or B.

MDF

MDF is also a type of engineered wood that can be used for different purposes. It is made by breaking down hardwood and softwood into fibers and combining them with resins and wax by applying high temperature and pressure to improve the texture. MDF is denser than plywood and can be used to create furniture and other projects that can withstand weather effects.

Compared to other engineered woods, MDF is very durable as is made to withstand the effects of water and weather.

OSB

OSB is the abbreviation for Oriented Strand Board, which is a wood created by combining different flakes and wood strands with adhesive. Each sheet is then compressed into a board. The sheets are made into mats with strong load bearing characteristics. Some OSB boards are sanded, while others are not; some OSB boards are moisture resistant, while others are not. Like plywood, you need to leave gaps for OSB too so that when it expands due to moisture, it has the space to do so. OSB is great for flooring and paneling.

LSL

LSL stands for laminated strand lumber and is created using small strips of wood that are arranged in an angled pattern and created by compression, which makes it very dense. It is very resistant to weight and torsion because of its angled pattern. The composition of LSL is 95% wood and 5% resin. However, it is not the first choice of wood workers due to its high cost.

LVL

Another type of engineered wood is LVL, or laminated veneer lumber, which consists of wood veneers bonded together with resins and adhesives, and then compressed under heat and pressure. It is considered a sustainable building material because it utilizes smaller, fast-growing trees and reduces waste by using wood veneers efficiently. It is exceptionally strong, even if primarily bears the load in one direction due to its single grain axis; since it can withstand heavy loads, is often used in structural applications such as beams and joists in residential and commercial construction. It is also used for window and door headers, as well as in the construction of engineered wood products like I-joists and roof trusses.

Chapter 2: The Language of Lumber

Understanding Lumber Grades

Understanding lumber grades is something crucial in the world of woodworking. Don't worry; I'll do my best to make it as easy as pie (or as easy as sawing a board, at least!)

You know, when you are at a lumberyard, you'll be surrounded by stacks of wood that all look similar each other.... and you start scratching your head, wondering how to be sure to choose the right pieces for your upcoming project. That's exactly when lumber grades come into play, because they are like those secret codes that tell you the quality of the wood you're about to buy.

Deciphering the Lumber Grade Code

So, what's this lumber grade code, you ask? As we have anticipated it is like the secret handshake of woodworking; the different grades are denoted by a mix of numbers and letters, let's break it down.

First things first, the quality of the wood determines the grade of the lumber. They will inform you if that wood is first-rate or merely adequate. You want the best for your initiatives, don't you think?

- **FAS (Firsts and Seconds):** FAS is comparable to the model student of the lumber industry. It is the highest-quality wood available and its name refers to it as "Firsts and Seconds," that is its full name. You may think of it as the wood version of a celebrity walking the red carpet. Wood that has been graded as FAS is clean, straight and free of significant flaws. It has a refined and sophisticated appearance, making it an excellent choice for projects in which the natural splendor of the wood should take center stage. You won't find a more beautiful kitchen table or a more heirloom-worthy cabinet anywhere else. Just for a moment, picture a dining table that is so spotless that you can't help but stare in awe at the wood grain: it is a fantasy that may now be accomplished using FAS wood.

- F1F (FAS 1-Face): F1F lumber indicates that one face of the board meets FAS requirements, while the other face may have some defects. This grade is still considered high quality.

- **Select and Better (SEL&BTR / SEL)** Even if it falls just a hair short of FAS standards, Select and Better is still pretty darn fantastic. In spite of the fact that it could have a few insignificant character markings, it is perfect for use in furniture and cabinets, both of which should have a clean and polished appearance. It's sharp and polished, much like a suit that's been expertly cut. Imagine you are building a streamlined and contemporary bookcase or a chic kitchen island. You may rely on Select and Better wood to be a reliable collaborator when fashioning those elegant items.

- **Common Grades:** The character of the wood is best seen in the common grades. I'm referring to things like knots, burls, and other unique characteristics. The more common grades are ideal for use in projects with a rustic aesthetic, like as log cabins or the fashionable farmhouse-style furniture. Just picture yourself creating a cozy coffee table with a top that is covered with intricate knots and swirls...it's a piece that brings a sense of history and coziness to whichever room it's in. We can find: 1 Common / 2A Common / 2B Common / 3A Common (the lowest grade)

Common Grading Associations

You may be asking who the referees for the lumber grade are at this point. The National Hardwood Lumber Association (NHLA) and the Western Wood Products Association (WWPA) are two examples of the types of associations that fall under this category. They act as a kind of quality control force for wood, ensuring that everyone adheres to the grading standards.

You'll frequently see the associations' stamps on the wood, which indicates that they adhere to their own unique sets of grading norms. If you see a stamp that has the NHLA or WWPA logo on it, you may be confident that the wood has been assigned the appropriate grade.

Please be aware that grading processes might differ somewhat from one location to another and from one specific grading authority to another. Always verify the grade stamp, and talk to your lumber supplier, to be sure you're obtaining the level of quality and grade you need for the tasks you're working on with wood.

Keep in mind that there is no response that is appropriate for everyone: whether you want to embrace the natural character of common-grade wood or go for the flawless finish of FAS, the decision ultimately comes down to the project at hand and your own sense of aesthetic.

Therefore, while you are at the lumberyard, keep an eye out for these grades, and choose the one that best fits the character of the project you are working on. You could wish to get that Select and Better if you plan on constructing a bookcase that is contemporary and chic. Choose the Common grade of wood, that features all those wonderful defects, if, on the other hand, you plan to construct a homey and rustic coffee table.

Don't be afraid of lower-grade wood! After all sometimes those knots and character marks can add so much charm to your project! And it's like giving your piece a story to tell.

In the end, try not to worry too much about the grades; instead, accept the peculiarities and use them into your woodworking voyage. They are just a guide to select the appropriate wood for your projects and guarantee that the finished products are ones of which you can be proud.

Lumber Dimensions and Sizing

The size game: Nominal vs. Actual Dimensions

As you walk through a lumberyard, you see dozens of wooden pieces of all shapes and sizes all around you. 1x2, 2x4, 4x8... it's like a numerical jigsaw puzzle. But fear not, we're here to demystify it all.

The fact is that those numbers on those boards aren't telling the whole truth, they're like the height listed on a dating profile; they're just not accurate! You have to understand that there are two types of timber dimensions: nominal and actual.

- The dimensions listed on the boards at the lumberyard are the **nominal dimensions**. They're like the wood's stage name. For example, a 2x4 board's nominal dimensions are, you guessed it, 2 inches by 4 inches.
- But the wood's true identity is hidden beneath the surface, in fact if you measure your 2x4 board, you'll find that it's actually around 1.5 inches by 3.5 inches. This is the **actual dimension**. It's like discovering your favorite actor isn't as tall as they claim!

You might be curious as to why lumber plays this size game. Well, it all dates back to the wood's journey from the forest to your project: when trees are harvested and milled, they shrink during the drying process. Therefore, the wood that was originally 4 by 4 inches becomes a board that is 3.5 by 3.5 inches.

Lumber Dimensions Cheat Sheet

Now, let's talk about some common sizes you will probably encounter during your woodworking voyage:

1. **2x4:** this is the superstar of the lumber world. It has a wide range of applications, is quite robust, and works well for framing. But keep in mind that its real dimensions are somewhere about 3.5 by 1.5 inches,
2. **1x6:** This one's perfect for projects where you need a wider board, like shelves or siding, even if, as you've probably guessed, it's more like 0.75x5.5 inches.
3. **4x8:** This giant can be your best friend for larger projects. Yes, you guessed it, it's approximately 3.5x7.25 inches.

A quick anecdote from my early woodworking days: I once made the mistake of purchasing what I believed to be a 2x6 board for a tabletop. You can probably figure out where I'm heading with this. When I measured it, I found that it was more along the lines of 1.5 inches by 5.5 inches. My table ended up a tad narrower than I'd envisioned, but it still turned out great.

Choosing the right size is like finding the perfect puzzle piece - it can make or break your project. Here are some tips:

- **Consider Your Design:** What does your project require? Do you need strength, width, or length? Understanding the requirements of your design can assist you in selecting the appropriate size.

- **Nominal vs. Actual:** Always keep in mind the difference between nominal and actual dimensions otherwise you will encounter bad surprises when you start cutting and building your project
- **Waste Not, Want Not:** Make sure you carefully plan out each cut to reduce the amount of wasted material. There is nothing more heartbraking than throwing away perfectly fine wood and adding it to the pile of waste.

Grain Patterns and Characteristics

Wood's Unique Fingerprint

Think of every piece of wood as a record of a tree's life. Like nature's fingerprints, the grain patterns, knots, and burls in a piece of wood may be used to reconstruct its history. Learning to recognize these traits is like being an expert biographer. Grain patterns reveal much about the character of the wood, they are what make each piece special and distinctive. The 3 most common grain patterns are as follows:

1. **Straight Grain (Long Grain):** Think of a forest where all of the trees are in a row. Wood with a straight grain contains fibers that run in the same direction along the length of the wood, giving it a clean and uniform look. It's like a well-organized library.
2. **End Grain:** You may think of end grain as a cross-section of tree rings. Look at the end of a board, and you'll notice this. These designs can be complex and interesting to look at. In this case the grain direction is perpendicular to the length of the board, and this wood is more porous and less structurally stable than long grain.

3. **Curly Grain (Cross Grain):** Often referred to as "figured grain," it is considered the rebel of the wood world. The surface is covered in whirling patterns that seem to dance together. It's the wood's way of saying, "I've got a wild side!" In this case the grain direction is diagonal or at an angle to the length of the board it can cause tear-out and instability.

Knots are like the freckles on wood's surface, considered imperfections by some woodworkers and at the same time seen as decorative traits by some others. We can identify 3 main types of knots:

1. **Pin Knots:** These are tiny, adorable knots that add a bit of rustic charm to anything you're working on.
2. **Sound Knots:** They're incredibly solid and won't fall out, adding a unique flair to any project. They are like the wood's beauty marks
3. **Dead Knots:** Dead knots are like the wood's scars. Over time, they could fall out, leaving a hole, however there is no need to be concerned about this because they may be filled with epoxy to create a magnificent aesthetic.

Grain direction, that basically refers to the orientation of the wood fibers within a piece of lumber, is something crucial for certain projects like tabletops and cabinet doors. If you understand well the concept of grain direction you can prevent your project from warping or cracking, because you will be able to work with the natural characteristics of wood.

It is essential for several reasons:

- **Minimizing Tension and Stress:** Changes in humidity and temperature cause wood to undergo both expansion and contraction. When you cut or shape wood in a direction that is perpendicular to the direction of its grain, you produce areas of tension and stress within the wood fibers; as a result of this strain, the wood may seek to revert to its normal, relaxed state, which may result in the wood warping or breaking.
- **Proper Joinery:** It is critical to align the grain direction when putting wood pieces together. When building a tabletop, for example, it's desirable to have all of the boards with the grain going in the same direction. This ensures consistent expansion and contraction, lowering the possibility of warping. You may run into issues if you combine boards with opposing grain orientations since they react differently to environmental changes.
- **Avoiding Cross-Grain Gluing:** When the grain of two pieces of wood runs in different directions, it might be difficult to glue the pieces together. As a result of the diverse methods in which the pieces of wood expand and shrink, there is a possibility that fractures or splits will appear between the pieces.
- **Ease of Workability:** Wood Cutting or shaping wood along the grain, as opposed to cutting or shaping against the grain, is typically the easiest way to deal with wood. Cutting across the grain of a piece of wood can result in splintering, tear-out, and a finish

that is uneven. (Tear-out is something that occurs when wood fibers are pulled out of the surface during cutting, leaving a rough and uneven finish).

- **Joinery:** Proper joinery often requires an understanding of grain direction. For example, when creating a mortise and tenon joint, it's fundamental to align the long grain of the tenon with the long grain of the mortise for obtaining the maximum strength possible.

When cutting or planing wood, "going against the grain" means doing so in a direction that is perpendicular to the natural orientation of the wood fibers or grain pattern. If you do it on purpose, you may produce interesting visual effects by drawing attention to the variations in the color of the wood, the grain patterns, or the texture. You may generate one-of-a-kind visual effects or draw attention to particular aspects of the design of a project by manipulating the grain direction on specific portions of the project.

Burls: Nature's Gemstones

Have you ever come upon burl wood? It's like discovering a long-lost treasure in the depths of the woods. Burls are the knobby growths that appear on trees and are responsible for producing some of the most captivating and desirable grain patterns. Imagine them as the treasures that nature has to offer. The use of burl wood in craft projects is analogous to fashioning works of art from the trunk of the tree.

When I was searching around a lumberyard one time, I came upon a burl slab that looked just like a piece of art. Even though it was a bit more expensive, I couldn't say no to the stunning originality of the item and in fact it is now a magnificent coffee table that I constructed out of it, in the center of my living room. Every time I take a look at it, it brings to mind the fantastic tales that wood has the potential to convey.

Chapter 3: Managing Defects and Flaws

Strategies for incorporating defects into your design

Just as a skilled sailor can spot subtle changes in the wind, a seasoned woodworker can identify common defects and flaws in wood. Here are some you may see:

1. **Knots:** As already discussed, there are several types of knots (pin knots, sound knots, and dead knots); Your work may benefit from having some sound knots, whereas dead knots could require some further work to be completed.

2. **Checks:** It might be difficult to identify checks since they sometimes lie hidden beneath the surface of the wood. Examine the surface for any fissures or fractures as small as a hair's breadth.

3. **Blemishes:** Examine the wood carefully for any blemishes, such as stains, discolorations, or dark areas. These flaws can have an effect on the aesthetic of the wood, but it may still be recoverable.

4. **Warping:** This is a term that refers to the wood cupping, twisting, bending, or crooking in some way. It's like being thrown into a storm at sea. Straightening out warped wood may need more time and work.

"Smooth seas do not make skillful sailors." Same story in woodworking. The following are some ways that may be used to include flaws into your design:

1. **Highlight Knots** - Rather than trying to hide them, embrace knots and use them as design components. They have the potential to become focal pieces or to lend an air of rustic charm to the project.

2. **Fill in checks** - If you find minor checks in the wood, you might want to consider filling them with epoxy glue or a wood filler whose color is similar to that of the wood. This not only fixes the issue, but it also injects some originality into the project.

3. **Employ ingenious camouflage techniques** by disguising flaws with well planned designs. Place a knot, for instance, at a location where it will organically mix in with the overall look of the project.

4. Minor blemishes - blemishes that aren't too noticeable may usually be sanded away or strategically positioned so that they don't take away from the overall beauty of the item.

5. Features That Make Your Project Unique - Bear in mind that what some people consider to be a defect, others regard as a quality that makes your project special. Don't be frightened to let your creative compass lead the way, it will never steer you wrong.

Just to give you a more practical example, some years ago, while I was working on a rustic dining table, I came upon a knot that was just too lovely to hide. Instead, I used it as the focal point of the table, drawing attention to the allure of its natural state. The knot not only served as a topic of discussion, but it also elevated a possible "defect" to the status of a prized feature.

When to Avoid Flawed Wood

In the same way that an experienced skipper will stay away of dangerous waters, there are instances when it's advisable to steer clear of flawed wood:

1. **Structural Integrity** - It is advisable to avoid utilizing a piece of wood for load-bearing components if the piece of wood has serious faults that undermine its structural integrity.
2. **Aesthetic Preferences** - It's alright to avoid flawed pieces that don't correspond with your design goals if you have a particular vision for your project that requires immaculate wood. This is the case if you have a specific vision for your project that requires pristine wood.
3. **The customer's Expectations** - If you are creating an item for a customer that has high standards for your work, it is imperative that you select a type of wood that can live up to those standards.
4. The intricacy and quality of the project should influence your decision about the type of wood to choose: **complex projects** should probably steer clear of wood that has large flaws, as they might make the crafting process more difficult.

Warping and Cupping

To begin, we need to have an understanding of the movement of wood.

Imagine the following: You are captaining a wooden ship out in the open ocean, and the size of your vessel shifts in response to the ebbing and flowing of the tides. Wood behaves in much the same way; it breathes and moves in response to the world around it. The success of your woodworking endeavors depends on your ability to master this dance.

Bear in mind the following things to take into account:

1. The Direction of the Grain Wood tends to expand and compress more across its grain than it does along its grain. Imagine this phenomenon as the expansion and contraction of the ship's hull as it moves through the water.

2. The effect of humidity - Variations in humidity can cause wood to either take in or give off moisture, which can result in either expansion or contraction of the wood. It's similar to how a sailor gets used to the motion of the ship by developing sea legs.

3. Diverse Woods, Diverse Movements - The amount of movement that may be expected from different species of wood varies greatly, for example hardwoods with a high density, such as oak, tend to be less mobile than softwoods such as pine.

Preventing and Correcting Warping

Now that we've deciphered wood's whims, let's discuss how to prevent and correct warping, that is analogous to keeping your ship steady in high seas. Warping can happen when wood dries unevenly or faces excessive moisture. Here's how to stay on course:

Start with lumbers that have been dried thoroughly. Since moisture content matters kiln-dried wood is your best choice. Keep the moisture content of your wood stable by storing it in an atmosphere that is under strict control. It is important not to subject one side to a higher relative humidity than the other. If you want to prevent moisture from entering or leaving your wood too rapidly after it has been cut, you should seal the cut ends.

If you catch the warping in its early stages, you may be able to repair it by dispersing the moisture in the material. When using a surface that is moist, it is best to position the concave side down so that there is uniform absorption. When dealing with warps that are difficult to remove, applying pressure in the opposite direction of the warp with weights or clamps might be helpful. It's similar like altering the sails on a ship in order to recover control of it. Heat and steam can be helpful for dealing with extreme warping. After the wood fibers have been pliable using an iron or steam generator, the surface may be flattened and reshaped.

Flattening Cupped Wood

Cupping occurs when the surface of your project takes on a curvature, similar to the way the deck of a ship does. Moisture-related wood movement is what causes wood to cup. In particular we can identify many causes that lead to this effect:

Moisture Inequality is certainly the main cause. As you know wood is hygroscopic, thus it may take in and give out moisture depending on the relative humidity around it. Uneven swelling and shrinking occur when one side of a piece of wood absorbs or releases moisture at a different rate than the other. If the top of a board absorbs moisture more quickly than the bottom, for instance, the top will expand at the expense of the bottom, resulting in cupping.

Moreover, we have to take in consideration the grain direction, in fact the orientation of the wood's growth rings or grain pattern plays a crucial role in cupping. Cupping typically occurs perpendicular to the growth rings: when moisture is absorbed, the wood's cells expand more across the width (tangentially) than along the length (longitudinally), and it is exactly this difference in expansion rates that causes the cupping effect.

We'll have cupping also if also if our lumber remains exposed to moisture sources on one side (think for example about rain or condensation): similarly, wood placed against a surface with different moisture levels (e.g., one side against a concrete floor) may also cup due to moisture transfer.

Also the initial drying process of freshly cut lumber is crucial, in fact wood may cup if it's not properly stacked and stickered (spaced apart) to allow for even drying. Uneven drying can result in moisture imbalances, and as we have seen this will lead to cupping.

The last scenario worth mentioning involves wood used indoors, like in furniture or cabinetry: this wood should be acclimatized to the indoor environment before use because if wood with a different moisture content is installed in an indoor space, it can later absorb or release moisture, leading to cupping.

Cupping has the potential to throw off the direction of your woodworking project, but do not panic! The following steps can help you return cupped wood to its original shape.

In order to evaluate the cupping, place a straightedge across the side that is concave: the depth of your cup is equal to the distance between the straightedge and the wood.

For mild cupping, place the concave side down on a damp surface and place weights on top, then allow the wood to absorb water until it flattens.

For more severe cupping, consider the use of a hand plane or power planer. Begin on the convex side and work your way down until flat.

Remember to maintain a consistent humidity level in your workshop to prevent future cupping...and don't make the same mistake as me! In my early woodworking days, I crafted a stunning wooden dining table. However, I made the rookie mistake of improper storage, and one day, I was greeted with a surprise: my table had developed severe cupping. It looked like a small wave frozen in time!

Why Straight Wood Matters

There's another anecdote from my early woodworking days, that easily clarifies the importance of straight wood. I was crafting a beautiful dining table for a dear friend. The design was impeccable, the wood was of high quality, and my excitement was through the roof. However, I made a critical error—I overlooked the importance of straight wood. As I began assembling the table, it quickly resembled a rollercoaster. One leg was longer than the other, and the top resembled a funhouse mirror. My dining table had become an abstract work of art, but it was completely impractical. I had to disassemble the entire project and start anew with meticulously selected, straight boards... The table came together flawlessly the second time around, and it still adorns my friend's dining room.

Using straight wood is fundamental, and the following reasons will explain why:

1. Faster and Easier Assembly: The boards are straight, so they go together like puzzle pieces. It's like putting together a ship with components that are an exact fit for each other; the process is incredibly streamlined.

2. Aesthetic Appeal: If you use warped wood, your masterpiece may end up looking like a Picasso painting—unique, but not necessarily in a positive manner. A smooth and expert finish may be ensured by using wood that is straight.

3. Stability and strength: Using straight wood as a basis for a project ensures that it will be strong and resilient. Imagine it as the keel of the ship you're building out of wood; it ensures that everything stays level.

How to Ensure Straightness

Now that you know why straight wood is so important, here are some tips to help you achieve it. Visit a lumberyard or hardware shop near you and carefully choose each board by hand. Examine it lengthwise for any signs of kinks, bows, or warps. To better see discrepancies, bring a straightedge or even a two-by-four and use it as a guide. Line it up down the board's length and check to see whether every corner makes contact. Third, remember to look at both ends of the board. Sometimes a board can look straight, but closer inspection will reveal a considerable bend or warp at one end.

Buying longer boards and chopping out the crooked bits is an option if you can't ind perfectly straight ones. This will help you keep your project straight and save usable wood.

Winding Sticks

What winding sticks are

Ingenious in their simplicity, winding sticks allow you check if a board is true and flat. They consist of two narrow, straight-edged sticks (often made of wood) and serve as your woodworking compass. When used correctly, they let you pick up on nuances you might have missed.

You're making a tabletop, and you have no idea that it looks like a roller coaster, that's the risk of boards with hidden twists, known as "winding." These invisible flaws might cause your furniture to wobble and your joinery to be crooked. Protect yourself from this woodworking nemesis with the help of some winding sticks as they expose the reality about your boards, allowing you to detect and fix any curvature before it ruins your work of art.

How to Use Winding Sticks

Using winding sticks is a straightforward process. Here's your step-by-step guide.

Materials You'll Need: Two identical, straight-edged sticks (winding sticks). They can be as simple as two wooden rulers or specially crafted sticks for this purpose; Your piece of wood that you want to inspect.

1. Place your board on a flat, level surface, like your workbench or a table. Be sure that it's adequately supported, so it doesn't rock or wobble.

2. Position the first winding stick at one end of the board, in a direction that is perpendicular to its length. Make sure it rests entirely on the surface.

3. Place the second winding stick to the opposite end of the board, making sure it is facing the same direction.

4. Now, here's the magic: stoop down and eye-level the sticks. You'll notice any discrepancies as gaps or misalignments between them.

- **Twisting to the Left:** in this case the stick should be higher on the left side; this means your board is winding or twisting in a counterclockwise direction.

- **Twisting to the Right:** In this case the stick is higher on the right side; this means your board is winding or twisting in a clockwise direction.

Once you've identified the winding direction, it's time to take action. You can flatten your board by planing or jointing it until the winding sticks align perfectly. This ensures your board is flat and ready for woodworking glory.

Tips for avoiding curved and twisted boards

Let's see a treasure trove of tips to keep your lumber straight and true.

1. Start with a Straight Edge:

When you are searching for the ideal board, you should always start by examining one of the board's edges. Put it down on a level surface, and check that all of its edges are clean and straight. In your search for straight lumber, this will serve as your north star and point you in the right direction. Keep in mind that a crooked edge is a solid indicator that danger is on the way.

2. Check for Twist:

Make sure there is no twist in the board. Twist is a crafty adversary that can transform an otherwise perfect board into a woodworking nightmare. To determine whether or not the board has twist, just place it on a level surface and examine it while holding it at eye level. A twisted board may be identified by the presence of one or more edges or corners that are raised slightly above the surface. Stay away from it!

3. Beware the Cup:

Cupping is another nemesis that can plague your woodworking adventures. A cupped board is like a potato chip, with its edges curving upward. To spot this problem, place the piece of wood on its narrowest edge and look for gaps between the board and the surface: if you see daylight peeking through, that board has a cupping problem.

4. Embrace Kiln-Dried Lumber:

Opt for kiln-dried lumber whenever possible, as this helps reduce moisture content, minimizing the chances of your lumber warping or twisting. It's like giving your wood a spa day, and who doesn't love a relaxed piece of lumber?

5. Invest in Quality Wood:

It is important to get excellent wood from trustworthy vendors. Even if it costs a little bit more, the assurance of quality and the peace of mind it provides are well worth the investment. The grain pattern of quality timber is typically more consistent and there are fewer defects in the wood, both of which make it simpler to deal with.

6. Let the Wood Acclimate:

Wood, much like a good wine, need some time to become used to its environment before it can be used. When you get your lumber back to your house, you should let it rest in your workshop for a few days before you use it. By allowing the wood to acclimatize to the humidity and warmth of your workstation over the course of this acclimation period, you will reduce the likelihood of unexpected twists and turns occurring.

7. Buy Extra:

In the unpredictability of carpentry, keeping additional lumber on hand is like to traveling on a lengthy journey with a spare compass. It acts as a safety net in the event that something goes wrong or the wood discloses defects that were previously hidden. If you have additional timber on hand, you may easily replace a piece that is giving you trouble without setting the whole job behind.

8. Work with Straight-Grained Wood:

As already discusses, straight-grained wood is the most reliable partner for your woodworking adventure, especially if you are a beginner: it is less likely to warp and twist and it is an excellent choice for projects in which stability is of the utmost importance

9. Joint and Plane to Perfection:

Even the greatest boards can sometimes display mild warping or cupping if they haven't been properly joint and planed. Don't lose hope; this is the perfect opportunity to show off your woodworking skills. Before beginning your project, you should first flatten the boards using jointing and planing procedures.

10. Don't Rush the Drying Process:

If you're dealing with newly sawn wood, avoid the impulse to rush into your job. The wood needs time to dry out properly before it can be used. When it comes to warping and twisting, green lumber that is still loaded with moisture behaves like a wild beast, so allow it to slowly dry in the air, or consider purchasing a moisture meter so you can keep track of its drying process.

11. Store Lumber Properly:

Ensure that your lumber is properly stored (even well-seasoned lumber can become unusable if it is improperly stored).

12. Master the Art of the Jointer:

A jointer is your secret weapon against twisted boards, therefore you should master the art of using it. You will be able to construct an accurate and level reference surface for your project if you joint the edges of the lumber you are using.

13. Get to Know Your Moisture Meter:

A moisture meter is your trusty navigator in the sea of woodworking. It enables you to measure the moisture content of your timber, allowing you to ensure that it is at the ideal level for the project you are working on. You might think of it as the personal fitness tracker for your wood.

14. Embrace the Art of Clamping:

While you're putting together your project, make use of clamps to bring any boards that aren't behaving properly into alignment. During the construction process, clamps serve the same purpose as the steady hand of a captain steering a ship through high seas; they ensure that everything remains in its proper location.

Chapter 4: Must-Have Woodworking Tools for Beginners

When you are a woodworker, your skills lie in your hands. Woodworking is an ancient art, and in the pre-industrial era, many people had a fundamental understanding of how to work with wood. When you learn to work with wood work, you acquire new skills and artistry, as well as being able to fix things around you. Moreover, basic woodworking skills provide you with an avenue to make some extra money on the side.

Today, as we rely more on artificial materials for much of our built environment, the skills of woodworking are revered and celebrated as the sign of a true craftsman. Nevertheless, we still depend on wood for a lot of furniture and fixtures. In addition, anyone can learn to work with wood, and this activity can make for a fun hobby or profession. It's certainly a valuable survival skill. As a carpenter or woodworker, you have to focus on the quality and nature of the wood and keep its natural characteristics in mind. Woodworkers should know about different kinds of wood and be able to choose the right one for each individual project. First, you need learn how wood behaves and how to operate on it. You have to know the proper orientation and cut for the board and the direction of the plane, and you have to know about the quality and grain of the wood so that you can work with the grain and not against it, which is what will enable you to create beautiful finishes. You must also take into account how the wood will behave under different conditions, such as moisture and heat.

Woodworkers should also know their tools very well, including how to sharpen them and keep them in the best condition. The secret to clean, easy woodworking is sharp, well-maintained tools. You should follow all of the maintenance and cleaning tips for your different tools if you want to use them to create good furniture. Treat your tools like your hands. If you do not maintain and sharpen your tools, you will only harm the project and yourself. Therefore, you need to learn the basic skill of sharpening and do it well regularly.

You should also know how to prep the wood for further work and how to finish it so that what you create presents a craft well mastered. The finish and the final beautification of a piece of furniture is as important as the whole process of creating it. You may put weeks of hard work into creating a piece, but if you don't use the right kind of tools and chemicals to finish it, it won't reach its full potential. There are many different finishes that you can achieve by hand.

Marking gauge

Marking gauges are a common woodworking tool that are used in both rough and fine joinery work. They have a locking mechanism that locks the gauge in place and keeps it from slipping. Thus, they enable you to make a measurement and then store it so that you can repeat the same measurement, precisely, as many times as you need. They are very necessary for making any kind of furniture.

Marking gauges are easy to use for multiple purposes, including mortise and tenon joints, dove tails, and rabbets. They are also helpful for tasks such as thicknessing.

The main purpose is to draw a line parallel to the reference edge to mark cuts and joints. Thus, it is one of the most important tools for joinery.

Different marking gauges are designed for different uses. The best one for beginners is the Robert Larson combination gauge, which has an easy, classic design and is good for many common woodwork and joinery tasks. The wood river wheel marking gauge is also a good choice because it is easy to use and feels great in the hand; it also makes precise measurement and cuts. These types of marking gauges allow you to create perfect measurements for joinery work.

Combination Square

A combination square is a very useful and versatile adjustable square that can be used to check boards and projects for squareness. It can also help you take precise measurements and make depth measurements and adjustments. It can create both 90- and 45-degree angle cuts, which are the most important cuts to make in woodworking and joinery.

The combination square should be used with a pencil to mark the edges and angles. However, for more precision and edge, you can use a marking knife to create markings.

Many brands make combination squares, and they all essentially do the same thing. However, you should make sure that you choose a good quality combination square because even a degree or two of deviation can create a bad measurement and lead to an unusable piece of wood because of a bad cut.

If you want to accept my suggestions, Irwin tools 12" combination square and Starrett 12" combination square offer the best balance of design, price, adjustment speed, and accuracy. You should also consider what is most comfortable for you.

Clamps

Clamps are required for almost all woodworking projects, and they have many other uses as well. When choosing the right clamps for a particular project, pay attention to the strength and weight management of the clamps. While clamps are simple, easy-to-use tools, the ease of adjustment and durability of different brands matters a lot.

These tools are very versatile and can be used for many purposes, but, basically, they are used to hold everything together. In woodworking, they are most often used to hold components together while the long-term joining solution, which might include glue, screws, or more, is being set. Clamps can also be used to hold a final work together for a final check before it is assembled. Good quality clamps are like a third hand at your workstation.

The clamps can fasten onto different surfaces and hold the two or three surfaces together.

There are many different types of clamps, but the most useful is probably the pipe clamp. You can change the length of the pipes attached to them so that they can fit different purposes. However, pipe clamps are very heavy, so you should also keep some bar clamps available for other purposes. If you are just starting your woodworking journey, you should buy some all-purpose bar clamps and pipe clamps. Consider a set of pipe clamps that can be used for larger builds and bar clamp set that is inexpensive but can handle a lot of pressure.

Handsaw

The humble handsaw is an essential woodworking tool. As an incredibly versatile hand tool, it can be used to create different cuts, and it also helps with delicate joinery work. Even in the age of power tools, the handsaw has its own charm and importance, and every woodworker should have at least one.

In order for your use of the handsaw to be beneficial, you must first take accurate measurements and mark the cut lines correctly. Then, make sure that you always grip the handle properly and adjust your grip according to your comfort level. While cutting, keep the wood at a good height to balance your force.

There are many types of handsaws on the market, including the Kataba and the double-sided Ryoba. The Kataba has a backless blade that can be used to create rip cuts, cross cuts, and diagonal cuts. The Ryoba is a double-sided blade that can be used to create rip cuts and cross cuts. Although the double-sided Ryoba handles well, you need a level of expertise to do so safely and comfortably; thus, it is not recommended for beginners.

Smoothing plane

Smoothing planes are a very important tool for woodworkers because they are used to smooth and plane out wood for any kind of furniture or other element that requires a smooth finish. Smoothing planes are a kind of bench plane that have been around since the 17the century. Moreover, they are the last plane used in a woodworking project, as they remove the fine surface shavings to create a smooth finish. Using a smoothing plane to smooth out the wood is a good alternative to sandpaper because you can get the same results in a much shorter frame of time.

This tool should be used after wood has been flattened and smoothed by other bench planes. Smoothing planes can remove marks and uneven texture from a whole project that has been created with a machine.

Choosing a smoothing plane can be difficult because you need to balance the quality and price with the weight and hand feel, which are hard characteristics to determine when you're just a beginning woodworker. Even if there are many types of the smoothing planes, the Stanley Sweetheart No. 4 and the Lie Nielsen No. 4 are both recognized as industry standards for quality.

Mallet

A mallet is a great beginner's tool because it can be used for many different purposes. A mallet is a hammer-like tool with a broad head that can be used to drive another tool into the wood for carving and other purposes. It is also good for hitting wood broadly, without causing marring. The mallet is often made of rubber or wood and imparts a widely balanced force (in woodworking, wooden mallets are generally used). Wooden mallets are used to knock pieces of wood together or to put a force on the chisel or dowels; they do not deform the striking end of the metal tool, and they give you better control over the chisel.

If you are a beginner who wants to learn how to carve with a mallet, choose a mallet with a urethane head. You have to hold the mallet in such a way that you transfer all of your force into the chisel and not your hand, then tap on the chisel with the mallet head.

Chisel set

Chiselling involves the use of force to shape materials with a blade: a chisel is a tool with a cutting edge, characterized by a blade on the end of the handle, that can be driven into wood and used to carve, join, shape, and pare wood and to create intricacy and detail. A chisel has to be sharpened, held at an angle, and driven into the wood with the help of a mallet, which enables you to control the amount of force you put on the chisel.

There are many different types of chisel sets: the bench chisel is a very common and inexpensive type of chisel that is used in combination with a mallet; another type is a paring chisel, which have longer blades and handles; a mortise chisel is used to make holes in wood

In my opinion the best chisel sets on the market are the Narex 6-piece chisel set and the Irwin Marples 6-piece chisel set because of their durability and blade edges. It's always a good idea to buy chisels in sets because the different pieces are appropriate for different wood-working actions. You also want to consider the handle when choosing chisels and look for beginners' kits that are affordable and utilitarian.

Sharpening stones

Sharpening stones are also called whetstones, and they are used to create sharp edges on knives and chisels. They come in different materials and sizes: for instance, they can be made from naturally quarried material or artificially sourced composite material, they can have a flat edge for sharpening flat edges or complex edges for sharpening other tools.

All cutting and shaping tools for carpentry and wood work will need some sharpening from time to time, that's the reason why whetstones are so if you want to maintain the quality and sharpness of your tools.

Using it is quite simple: put the tool edge on the sharpening stone at an angle of 20 to 25 degrees, and place your fingers and thumb on the blade. Be careful not to hurt yourself in the process. Move the blade across the stone with even pressure, and maintain the angle.

There are many types of sharpening stones, but the best ones for wood working tools are water stones and diamond plates: water stones come with different types of grit and are meant to be used with water. However, these are naturally occurring stones, and the center will wear out over time, becoming concave when used frequently. If you are looking for a better option that will last longer than water stones, go for a diamond plate (yes it is expensive, but it is well worth the investment - it will last for decades without any issue!).

Circular saw

The circular saw is a power tool to which different kinds of circular blades can be attached to cuts through different materials. This type of saw was invented in the 18th century. The cutting action of a circular saw is different from that of other handsaws, as it occurs via rotation: the cut you'll obtain is very distinct and smooth in finish. Moreover, circular saws cut straight and are relatively accurate.

If you are a beginner, you definitely want to keep a circular saw in your work space, as the saw blade helps to ensure that you make the perfect cross cuts and rip cuts.

When you first start working with a circular saw, you should use a clamp or vise to hold the wood steady. The saw should be moved slowly across the wood at an able. As each tooth of the blade moves through the wood, the tooth makes a chip and cuts the wood.

There are different types of circular saws, including abrasive saws, biscuit joiners, brush cutters, flip over saws, concrete saws, cold saws and carbide saws, all of which are designed to cut through different materials. The type of saw you use really depends on the type of blade and technique you prefer and what you are planning to build. In other words, the project determines the saw.

It's best to buy an efficient, lightweight, versatile and economical saw that works well with different materials. You can also choose to buy a corded or cordless model depending on your preference. Always choose a saw that is built well and easy to maneuver.

Router

A router is a good power tool to go with your circular saw. In fact, a power router is one of the most versatile power tools you can have as a wood worker. It is used to cut, trim and shape wood, and it is made of multiple parts, including an electric motor, base, two handle knobs, and different kinds of bits for cutting through materials. Routers can be used for cabinet and shelving work, as well as storm window edges and weather stripping, as they can create circles and ovals with smooth round edges.

Depending on the tip attached, a router can do all sorts of things. For example, it can create smooth and perfect edges on a narrow piece of wood, replicate one type of cut on different pieces of wood, carve decorative molding and intricate patterns, and cut slots for support.

Here are some common types of routers:

1. **Fixed Base Router:** This one is relatively simple to use and offer consistent depth adjustments; it has a stationary base that provides stability during routing and it's suitable for precise and controlled cuts, making it ideal for tasks like edging and grooving.

2. **Plunge Router:** Plunge routers have a spring-loaded base that allows you to plunge the bit into the material, making it suitable for tasks that require starting a cut from the middle of a piece of wood. They are versatile and can handle a variety of tasks, including mortising and dado cutting.

3. **Combo Router Kit:** These kits include both a fixed base and a plunge base that can be interchanged, providing flexibility and versatility in one tool. They are the perfect choice for those woodworkers who want the advantages of both fixed and plunge routers without purchasing two separate tools.

4. **Trim Router:** Trim routers are compact and lightweight, making them perfect for smaller tasks such as trimming edges and making delicate, detailed cuts. They are easy to maneuver and control, making them a favorite among DIY enthusiasts and for adding decorative touches to woodworking projects.

5. **CNC Router:** Unlike hand-held routers, CNC (Computer Numerical Control) routers are computer-controlled machines used for precision routing and carving. They are popular in large-scale woodworking and manufacturing, where accuracy and repeatability are essential.

6. **Table-Mounted Router:** These routers are designed to be mounted on a router table, in order to provide stability and precision. These tools allow you to move the material over the stationary bit, making it easier to achieve consistent cuts, and are often used for tasks like molding, joinery, and edge profiling.

7. **Palm Router:** Palm routers, also known as mini routers, are compact and easy to handle with one hand. They are suitable for light-duty tasks such as rounding over edges and making small decorative cuts. Their small size makes them highly maneuverable in tight spaces.

8. **Heavy-Duty Router:** These routers are larger and more powerful, capable of handling demanding tasks such as deep grooving, large panel work, and heavy-duty profiling. They are commonly used in professional woodworking shops.

9. **Laminate Trimmer:** Laminate trimmers are designed specifically for trimming laminate surfaces and are often used in countertop installation and similar applications. They are small, lightweight, and easy to control.

10. **D-Handle Router:** D-handle routers have a handle shaped like the letter "D," providing a firm grip and better control. They are commonly used for edge profiling and other tasks requiring precision and maneuverability.

Power drill

Power drills are great tools for woodworking, as well as for other DIY projects and home repairs. A power drill rotates a drill bit to make a hole in plastic, metal, wood, and more. Its parts also include a handle, safety latch, trigger, and reverse switch, as well as has torque adjustment and a chuck that holds the drill bit in place. There are different tips for different purposes, including a screwdriver tip for driving screws into surfaces and join surfaces.

For example, with a power drill you can assemble furniture that come with DIY tags or to drill holes to hang picture frames, but you could also use it to mix paint and to sand round edges quickly. A power tool is just an excellent all-around tool!

Of course the type of power drill you have to use depends on your requirements and the types of material that you are working with. Among the different types we can find: impact drivers tighten or loosen screw bits and bolts; hammer drills have a hammering action to support work like masonry; rotary drills are another kind of drill; they have a rotator function and can be used to drill into concrete and masonry; cordless drills are a compact, easy-to-handle, and battery-operated option for creating holes and driving screws. If you are a beginner, I recommend starting with a cordless ones like Bosch power drills and choose one that comes with a case and different bits. The drill should be lightweight but powerful enough to get the job done.

Random orbital sander

A random orbital sander, also known as a palm sander, is a handheld power tool that sands in an orbiting motion, creating irregular overlapping circles. Invented in 1968, it is better than a belt sander and can be used to create different and finer wood finishes, perfect for preparing your project for painting.

You fix a sanding round pad to the vibrating mechanism, and the ball bearing allows the pad to rotate randomly; when the pad encounters hard points on the surface, it goes in a random orbital motion, polishing the wood as it moves.

There are different types of random orbital sanders to choose from, and you can choose based on the type of handle and grip the sander offers for proper sanding. Look for an economical option that works with different types of materials. It could be useful also to choose one that has variable controllable speeds, which will allow you to create the best kind of finish for different materials.

These tools are just a fraction of the numerous instruments at a woodworker's disposal. In upcoming sections, we will delve into additional tools specific to various woodworking techniques.

Chapter 5: Safety Measures For Your Workspace

How to choose your workspace

While dealing with woodworking, it is essential to ensure your security and safety measures of the surrounding environment. Therefore, the whole security issue begins with setting up your workshop.

Just as it applies to all forms of skills and creativity, a workspace is significant to woodworking: the workshop is close to being everything as it plays a large role in determining how much would get stored and how much production would be possible. As a result, it is only essential that you know what to watch out for when choosing and designing your workspace. As an amateur, deciding on a workspace can be pretty difficult, as several factors come into play, from space and location to your craft's specialty, among others. However, the key to finding the ideal workspace starts with noting what is most important to these crafters while working, and likewise, what is most important to you.

This part of the book is all about taking you through all that is essential for you as a woodworker as you create your beginner-friendly workspace.

Before setting up a wood shop, the location must first be determined. Of course, as a beginner, the most logical decision is to start small in an organized fashion. Luckily, you do not need to get a plot of land or rent an apartment for the sole purpose of your working space: a woodworking space can vary from a shed or a garage to a basement. As a beginner, it is only sensible that you start with something large enough to contain your productions but small enough not to be a waste of resources since you would not be involved in as much activity as an experienced woodworker.

The first option to most likely surface in your mind is of course your home; the major question would then be, "what part of my house should I adopt as my workshop?" But before we go into that, we shall cover the key essentials every woodworker must be on the lookout for when it comes down to choosing a workspace.

The Entrance

While dealing with woodworking, we cannot underestimate the importance of the entrance to the wood shop; a typical woodshop entrance might be as crucial as the space in it, because it is the only way through which everything, including power machines, raw materials, and basic tools can get through and into your workspace. Besides, people too, use that space to access your workshop. While the wood size coming in may not be the greatest factor in selecting a wide doorway since a larger wood piece can be cut before entering your workspace, the main determinants are the machines.

Maybe you will not use high-capacity tools from the beginning, but probably you'll decide to buy someone of them later in your woodworking journey; as a result, the entrance to your workspace must be large enough to take in these tools: room about to be converted into a woodwork workshop should be able at least to admit a tool of 32 inches in breadth (this is because companies now build tools capable of fitting into home spaces with doors of this breath due to an increasing number of home-based workspaces for woodworkers).

Note that attention need not be placed specifically and solely upon doors but on doorways in general. Doorways, I mean the space in front of doors, contribute to the entrance as well. You should not have stairs or other components that could potentially serve as a hindrance.

The Lighting

Every worker needs light, but the woodworker needs light a lot more than any other type of professional!
Woodworking workspaces depend largely on the lighting of the room in order to avoid as many injuries and casualties as may arise from the unavailability of light while working with dangerous tools. It is recommended to have enough natural light coming in even without electricity, even if electric additions must be present in any case; bulbs that give more natural light should be installed as they blend in without confusion and enhance clarity in the workspace.

Any woodworking shop, be it on a small scale or not, requires electricity for both powering machines and, as mentioned before, providing adequate lighting. Once the lighting has been taken care of, what ensues is the installation of electrical sockets. It is important to ensure the installation of sockets that meet your machine's needs, in other words, with the right amount of voltage to power your devices. Smaller machines will require smaller voltage, and bigger machines will require larger voltage for operation. While on the electrical aspect, keep provisions for multiple sockets to allow plugging in two or more machines at a time if need be. Because electricity is electricity (and not woodworking), a good idea is to invite an electrician to help you install all the needed electrical items, you just need to explain him what you want your final outcome to be!

Ventilation and Dust Collection

Except for workspaces belonging to woodworkers who don't mind inhaling the bulk of carcinogenic substances produced, dust collection is always essential! When selecting a location, it's important to consider the amount of dust you are likely to generate and how it might impact your surroundings. If your woodworking has no sawing of any kind or has little to no dust production involved, then you might not need to worry as much, but in general the dust and residue from cutting, shaving, and scraping must be cleared up to clean the air and keep the shop safety. For this purpose, various types of ventilating systems are available. As an indoor woodworker, get ready to invest in a quality dust vacuum.

Noise

If you plan to carry out your activities inside your home, you must consider the amount of noise you generate. Woodworking power tools generate ear-piercing noise when in use: the loudness and intensity of the sounds are so high that all woodworkers keep safety headphones on while working to prevent hearing damage. Alternatively, you can consider the use of earplugs.

If your woodworking has power tools involved, you will have to either move out or install sound insulation to whichever part of the house you choose to become your workspace. Also, make sure that no one enters your workspace while you are working.

We have discussed the key factors that you should take into account when selecting your workspace location. The unmentioned factor here is cost. But the issue of cost will depend largely on you. How much of the renovations can you afford?

After mentioning all these, we must emphasize that a workspace doesn't necessarily have to be a dedicated room. Your specific activity is what determines what type of workspace you need. If you are a simple carver working on small, plain objects, you won't require as many resources as a furniture maker would. Workspaces can be as simple as a bench, a portion of a room, or a sturdy cupboard or cabinet.

Also, as a beginner, especially if you're pursuing woodworking as more of a hobby than a commercial venture, it is perfectly okay to start with a scanty workspace as long as it serves your needs and gets your activities done. Strictly avoid wasting resources or spending money unwisely on items you most definitely do not need.

The best advice for a beginner would be "start small, start compact, but start, and then grow"!

Considerations About Safety

Creating a secure workspace in your woodworking journey is like building a fortress for your creativity. Think of it as your woodworking sanctuary, your own realm of sawdust and dreams. But unlike the knights of old, your most formidable adversary won't be a fire-breathing dragon but rather a lack of safety measures. So, let's armor up and secure our workshop castle!

Picture yourself donning a full set of protective gear before entering your woodshop: first of all you will have safety goggles that, like a medieval visor, will shield your eyes from flying wood chips, while earplugs will be like a trustworthy helm, protecting your hearing from the sound of power tools. Don't forget to protect your hands from splinters and other hazards by donning a pair of gauntlets, or robust work gloves.

Your tools are your most devoted sentinels, but they need to be organized like an army. Make sure that every tool has a specific location, whether it be on your workstation, in a holster on your tool belt, or on a rack that is mounted on the wall, like a knight who has a strong eye for detail. Remember that our biggest enemy is chaos in the workshop, which may lead to tripping hazards and misplaced tools that can wreak havoc on your project.

Now I want to mention the importance of having enough clear space during your woodworking operations.

Imagine a moat of clean space surrounding the place where you will be working. This area functions as a buffer between you and any undesirable visitors, just like water would protect a fortress. Keep the area clear of debris and obstructions and ensure that it is not congested. If you were to trip over a stray piece of timber at a crucial point in your project, it would be the same as if you had inadvertently lowered the drawbridge when you had intended to keep it raised. You definitely don't want that to happen!

Speaking of drawbridges, consider your workshop's electrical system. We can see electrical safety as the drawbridge that connects your castle to the outside world, so be sure to have extension cords and power outlets always in good condition without any frayed cable or loose connection. Equip your castle with ground fault circuit interrupters (GFCIs) for added protection against electrical hazards.

Moreover, an adequate ventilation is essential, as it protects against the toxic vapors that are released by paints, stains, and finishes. Ensure that fresh air circulates freely and continuously! You could also protect your lungs by wearing a respirator or dust mask when woodworking.

In general, and I think this is the simplest, but also the most effective (and underestimated) advice, be always prudent. Never allow your hurry to put your safety at risk. In the same way that going headlong into war is a formula for disaster, rushing through a project is also a prescription for disaster. Take things slowly, pay attention to any safety instructions, and make patience one of your guiding virtues.

The woodworking commandments

In your quest to secure your woodworking sanctuary, you must also familiarize yourself with the laws of the workshop. These are the commandments that every woodworker must follow, the code of conduct that ensures safety and order.

The Law of Proper Training - In the same way that a squire learns under the tutelage of an experienced knight, a woodworker should never begin their journey without first receiving the appropriate training. Before beginning more difficult tasks, you should first gain knowledge from more experienced woodworkers, study instructional videos, and practice your abilities, as it is imperative that you develop your woodworking skills in the same manner that a knight practices their swordsmanship.

The Commandment of Tool Respect - Tools are your loyal allies, your trusty companions in this creative battlefield, so please always respect them, since they have the power to create both order and chaos; this mean that you should keep them sharp and in good condition at all times, exactly like a knight's sword. If you give them the attention they need, they will continue to be loyal to you!

The Rule of Controlled Chaos – I know that sometimes the workshop takes on the appearance of a battleground, but it's essential that you become able to maintain what is called a "controlled chaos". Try to keep your workstation as neat and uncluttered as possible, and remove any sawdust or wood scraps regularly. The more organized your workstation is, the less likely it is that you will trip over anything or lose track of an important item.

The Decree of Emergency Preparedness - You need to be ready for any emergency that may arise, just like a knight getting ready for an unexpected battle. Always have a first-aid kit close at hand and be familiar with how to utilize it. Create a strategy for dealing with unexpected events, including a list of exits in the event of a fire. Your first and foremost concern should always be your safety.

The Covenant of Cleanliness - Maintain a regular sweeping schedule in your workshop to remove dust and dirt: not only does keeping your work area neat and tidy reduce the risk of mishaps, but it also makes it easier for you to think straight, much like a brave warrior who enters battle with a clear head.

The Oath of Tool Selection - Choose your equipment carefully: not every tool can be used for every kind of job, so choose the appropriate one for the current task to maximize both productivity and protection; this is comparable to choosing the appropriate armor and weapon for a certain adversary.

The Pledge to Learn from Mistakes - Even the bravest knights are human and will make mistakes, but they will grow stronger because of their missteps. When dealing with wood, mistakes can be seen as learning opportunities. Consider what went wrong, make the necessary changes to your methods, and move forward. The only way to achieve mastery is to learn from your mistakes. Personally, I lost count of how many mistakes I made early in my career! The point is: don't get discouraged! Success is around the corner!

Chapter 6: Measuring, Marking, and Layout

The Art of Measurement

Measurements are more than simply numbers on a tape measure; they are the bedrock of precision carpentry. The success of any DIY project, from a delicate jewelry box to a solid dining table, is entirely dependent on the accuracy of your measurements.

The first step is to pick the appropriate measurement tool. Think about how big and varied your project is: a flexible tape measure may be the finest ally for detailed, miniature work, while a firm measuring stick or ruler may be more appropriate for bigger projects.

Now that you have your implement, you can get to know your wood up close and personal. Keep the measuring device flush with the surface of the wood, carefully checking for overlaps and gaps that might cause mistakes. Accuracy is born from a deep familiarity between tool and material.

Let's speak about how holding steady is so crucial now. Hold the measuring device firmly but not too tightly, since too much pressure might cause inaccurate results. Your measures will hold up better with a gentle touch.

The seasoned woodworkers all agree on this one: always start your measurements at the same end of the tape because, if this pattern is maintained, the potential for mistakes to accumulate over time is diminished.

Finally, take your time when measuring. Remember the ancient saying, "measure twice, cut once," and take your time.

The "Hook" Technique: Precision at the Edge

Try to picture this: You've finally arrived at your woodshop, where you can focus on your latest creation. Your trusty tape measure hangs by your side, and the raw material, wood, is ready to be transformed. The "Hook" Method comes into play at this point.

In woodworking, the "Hook" Technique is a simple yet fundamental method as it guarantees that your measuring devices are as accurate as a Swiss watch. Where does the magic happen? Think of the hook that hangs off the end of your measuring tape, it's designed to catch the edge of your material, allowing you to start measuring from the very edge of your material.

There is no room for mistake with this method: there is no space for error or approximation when hooking onto the wood's edge. This precise measurement will guarantee that your work will be completely aligned. The "Hook" Technique is like a compass for woodworkers, leading them to precise measurements and beautiful results.

Avoiding Parallax Errors: The Illusion of Inaccuracy

Now let's talk about the devious trickster known as parallax error. Consider aiming a camera at an object from different angles; the object appears to shift position. If you're not cautious, this optical illusion might seep into your woodworking measures as well.

When your eye isn't perfectly aligned with the object you're measuring, you'll make a mistake known as parallax. It's as if your perspective is off just a hair, giving you skewed results and the results can be terrible, including misaligned joints, broken pieces, and a general feeling of annoyance in your private space for creativity.

When collecting measurements, keep your eye absolutely level to prevent parallax mistakes. Line up your eye with the ruler or tape measure. In your mind's eye, the measuring tool, and the target point should all be aligned in a straight line.

The Golden Ratio Unveiled

The Golden Ratio is an irrational mathematical constant, usually denoted by the Greek letter Phi (Φ), with a numerical value that is approximately 1.61803398875; in any case in woodworking it's not about the digits, it's about the magic it brings to your projects.

In its simplest form, the Golden Ratio can be defined as a proportion where the ratio of the whole to the larger part is the same as the ratio of the larger part to the smaller part. It sounds a bit confusing, doesn't it? The first time I heard this concept, I was baffled and couldn't understand what on earth math had to do with woodworking.

Let's break it down.

Imagine a line that is cut into two different parts, A and B, that are not equal. The Golden Ratio is present when the ratio of the entire line (A + B) to segment A is the same as the ratio of segment A to segment B. Mathematically, it can be expressed as:

$(A + B) / A = A / B = \Phi$

Now, why exactly is this number held in such high regard in the world of woodworking and design? Because it has an extraordinary talent for establishing proportions that are attractive to the eye. The Golden Ratio appears frequently in the natural world, as well as in art and architecture, and even in carpentry.

Imagine that you are building a table out of wood. You may use the Golden Ratio to figure out the optimal proportions for the tabletop, legs, and other components by applying the ratio. It is possible to create a piece that is not only useful but also visually harmonious if the process is carried out correctly.

The spiral pattern found in a nautilus shell is a typical inspiration for designers working in the furniture industry. Its alluring and beguiling look is the result of its chambers expanding at a rate that is proportional to the Golden Ratio. When dealing with wood, you may use the same guiding concept to determine the shape of chair legs, the proportions of a jewelry box, or the measurements of a bookcase, among other things.

So, how can woodworkers practically employ the Golden Ratio? Here are a few tips:

1. **Proportional Design**: When figuring out the sizes of the different components of your project, the Golden Ratio is a useful resource to use. For example, if you are building a wooden frame for a painting, you might want to think about applying the ratio to the width and height dimensions of the frame.

2. **Divine Dividers**: Golden Ratio calipers, also known as Fibonacci calipers, are specialized tools that help you proportion your designs accurately. They make it possible for you to determine exact points of division on the workpiece you are working on.

3. **Spacious Shelves**: You may use the golden ratio to establish the amount of space that should be left between shelves that you create. This guarantees that each shelf is not only practical, but also visually appealing.

4. **Drawer Dimensions**: Applying the Golden Ratio to drawer dimensions can result in drawers that are easy to open and have an aesthetically pleasing height-to-width ratio.

5. **Design Harmony**: Consider using the ratio to guide the curvature of wood components like chair arms or table legs in order to give them an harmonious feel.

Even while the Golden Ratio is a useful tool, it is essential to avoid falling into the trap of making it your master. The art of woodworking encourages both individual expression and creative problem solving. When done creatively, rule-breaking can result in stunningly original and stunningly beautiful creations.

Consider the Golden Ratio to be a reliable companion on your path through the world of woodworking. It is there to give direction, but it does not define how every action should be taken. Experiment, listen to your gut, and when the time is right, draw upon the enchantment of the Golden Ratio to craft carpentry creations that are not only useful but also visually enchanting.

Pencil Lines vs. Knife Lines

Imagine that you are ready to make an important cut on a piece of walnut that is just stunning. The margin for error is thinner than a carpenter ant's mustache hair. In situations like this, the age-old question of whether to draw lines with a pencil or a knife comes into play.

Pencil lines, which are the recognizable graphite streaks that we all grew up with, are easy to apply but occasionally result in lines that are, well, a touch too shaky. It's possible that you believe you're making straight cuts along that line, but the wood has other plans for you. It's like attempting to tap dance on a banana peel while wearing tap shoes.

At this point, using a utility knife or marking knife that is extremely pointed, you will incise a line into the wood fibers. It's the equivalent of telling the wood, "I'm coming through, whether you like it or not." The sharpness of a knife line provides an unusually gratifying sense of satisfaction. It's like woodworking's way of saying, "Yeah, I've got this."

Story Sticks

Let's move on to the tale sticks. No, these are not the props for a story to be told around the campfire. They are handy little aids that rescue you from the problem of having measures that aren't consistent with each other. A tale stick is just a piece of wood (it can be scrap) that you mark with all your critical measurements for a project. You use this to help you complete the work.

Suppose you are in the process of constructing a bookshelf that has several levels and each shelf needs to have very accurate spacing between them; you use your story stick to measure each shelf instead than measuring them individually and running the risk of making several little mistakes that may ultimately result in shelves that are not level. On the stick, you make your markings according to the specific dimensions for one shelf; after that, you just transfer those marks to the actual piece. There you go, each of your shelves is precisely where it should be.

"Bump and Shift" Technique

Ever had one of those moments when your freshly cut piece of wood doesn't fit into the puzzle like it's supposed to? You're not alone; we've all been there. That's where the "bump and shift" technique can be a game-changer. Consider for example the following situation: you've got a mortise and tenon joint, but the tenon seems to have stage fright and won't slide into the mortise. Instead of hammering away and hoping for the best (which usually ends in tears), you employ the "bump and shift": gently nudge the piece in the right direction – the bump – and then give it a little wiggle – the shift. It's like the woodworking equivalent of persuasion without the drama.

Workpiece Reference Faces

Now, let's speak about the workpiece reference faces, which, if ignored, may cause a lot of trouble. These are the unsung heroes of woodworking; they labor in the background to make sure everything is aligned properly.

Consider a tabletop made of several pieces of wood. They probably won't fit correctly if you just slam them together. The trick is to pick one side of each board as the reference. This is the side that will become the joining point for the final, seamless product. It maintains harmony, much like a conductor does in an orchestra.

Achieving perfect squareness

3-4-5 Method

You're making a stunning wooden frame for a piece of artwork or a mirror, and I suppose the last thing you want is for it to hang crookedly on the wall when it's finished! The 3-4-5 approach comes to the rescue to save the day in this particular situation.

Imagine that you are making a "L" shape on your piece of wood by drawing a right angle on it. Take 3 measurements along one edge, 4 measurements along the other edge, and 5 measurements across the diagonal. If those diagonal measurements align perfectly, congratulations, you've got yourself a square angle! If not, a little adjustment might be in order.

Diagonal Measurements

Speaking of diagonals, let's explore the importance of measuring them: measuring the diagonals of a project that should be square, such as a table or a cabinet, might help you determine whether or not everything is in balance. Imagine that you are in the process of putting together a cabinet and that you have already built the frame. Take a diagonal measurement starting from one of the top corners and ending in the opposite bottom corner, and then repeat this process for the other diagonal. You have arrived in squareville if the two measures are identical, otherwise if they do not already, it is time to make some changes so that they do. By using this procedure, you can assure that the doors and drawers of your cabinet will shut correctly, without leaving any unattractive gaps.

In spite of all of your hard work, there may be occasions when the end result of your woodworking project is not quite up to your standards. It's alright; the important thing about woodworking is not to learn how to avoid making mistakes, but rather how to correct them. Consider for a moment that you are constructing a box out of wood. After measuring the diagonals of your construction and seeing that they are not even, you come to the conclusion that it is not as square as you had hoped. There is no reason to freak out! Apply some little pressure to one of the corners while removing the pressure from the other corner. It's almost like a soft persuasion, like someone is saying to your wood, "Come on, be square!" Patience is a virtue in woodworking, as it is likely that you may have to go through this procedure more than once.

Precision Techniques for Angles

Dividers and Compasses

Have you ever imagined crafting a masterpiece with intricate patterns on a circular tabletop? The use of dividers and compasses is where the magic happens when it comes to crafting these types of projects: these unsung heroes of woodworking geometry are similar to reliable guides that will lead you through a complex maze of accuracy.

When your project requires even intervals and markers that are properly spaced apart from one another. you may create a captivating dance of accuracy and creativity with dividers by adjusting the width between the points, then delicately gliding them down the wood. This will provide the desired effect.

In addition, compasses are the tools of choice when it comes time to create circles. They are perfect for drawing circles of varying sizes thanks to the pencil that is attached to one end and the sharp leg that is attached to the other end of the tool. Imagine you are drawing circles inside circles, spiraling toward perfection as you use a compass to create a beautiful inlay pattern on your tables.

Miter Gauges

Woodworkers frequently find themselves in the process of searching for the perfect angle, whether it be for the purpose of creating attractive picture frames, obtaining immaculate joints, or adding a touch of elegance to their creations. So, here's a question: how do you create those impeccable mitered corners?

Enter miter gauges, which will serve as your reliable guides through the labyrinth of angles You may produce exact cuts at a variety of angles with the help of these tools, which function similarly to compasses in the realm of angles. Imagine for a moment that you are constructing an old-fashioned picture frame out of wood for a treasured family photograph: with a miter gauge, you can set it to the exact angle you desire – 45 degrees for a perfect right angle in this case – and guide your saw to create corners that would make a master carpenter nod in approval.

But here's the beauty of miter gauges: they're not limited to 45-degree angles. You can adjust them to any angle you need, opening up a world of possibilities for your woodworking projects. Whether you're crafting hexagonal boxes or triangular shelves, miter gauges are your golden ticket to angle perfection!

Bevel Gauges

Do you want to know how to accurately measure and reproduce angles that aren't the standard 90 or 45 degrees? Welcome to your new woodworking companions – bevel gauges!

For example if you want to build a one-of-a-kind bookshelf and you decide to give it a contemporary and distinctive edge by giving it angled edges, bevel gauges will prove to be your most reliable partners: they will assist you in accurately measuring the required angle, and after you have done so, you will be able to lock the measurement in place: this guarantees that you will be able to replicate it properly throughout all of your wood components, so ensuring a snug fit and an aesthetically pleasing end product.

But bevel gauges are also an additional tool that you will need in order to fashion woodworking items that have lovely beveled edges. Beveling gives a piece of simple wood the appearance of depth and dimension, so converting it into a genuine work of art. Imagine a gorgeous mirror frame with beveled edges that reflects light and lends an air of refined elegance to any space.

The Art of Scribing

What is Scribing in Woodworking and What is its Purpose?

First things first, what exactly is scribing in woodworking, and why is it such a valuable technique? Scribing is the art of fitting a piece of wood precisely to an irregular or uneven surface. It's like woodworking magic that allows you to conquer challenging scenarios where standard measurements and cuts fall short.

Consider the following example: you want to install a beautiful wooden countertop in your kitchen, and of course you want it to snugly fit against the wall...but the wall isn't perfectly straight, there are curves, bumps and other imperfections. Scribing is what saves the day in this situation. It allows you to construct a piece of custom-fitted wood that follows every shape of the wall and does not leave any unsightly gaps.

Another example from a very common scenario: baseboard trim. It is not uncommon for baseboards to come into contact with floors that are not level, corners that are not quite square, and walls with different imperfections. Now, of course I think you want to make sure that the baseboard trim you installed is sitting flush against the wall and the floor, without any gaps or strange angles to be seen. So, let's apply the scribing technique!

Just follow these steps:

1. **Prepare your trim:** To begin, cut your baseboard trim pieces to the length that you wish, being sure to leave some extra length for scribing.
2. **Position the trim:** Keep your piece of trim in place as you try to line it as closely as possible with the wall and the floor. It won't be a perfect match, but that's where the scribing comes in to work its wonders.

3. **Scribe the contour:** Using a compass or scribing tool, adjust it so that it follows the imperfections of the wall, and then trace the curves of the wall onto the trim piece. This results in the irregularities of the wall being transferred onto the wood.

4. **Cut along the scribe line:** Proceed with extreme caution as you cut along the scribed line that you've established. Because of this specific cut, your trim will be able to fit securely against the uneven wall, resulting in a flawless finish.

Scribing Cabinets

Installing cabinets is the next tough step in our woodworking project, so let's get started. Whether it's for a kitchen remodel or a storage solution that's been constructed specifically for the space, cabinets frequently need to be able to fit into areas that have uneven walls or flooring. Scribing is able to assist you once again, providing a professional and trouble-free installation for you.

Here is a step-by-step guide to scribing cabinets like a pro:

1. Place the cabinet in its designated place, making sure that it is level and plumb before doing so. There will be spaces between the cabinet and the wall; nevertheless, you need not be concerned since we will fill such gaps.

2. Scribe **the contours:** Take your reliable compass or scribing instrument and draw the imperfections of the wall onto the side of the cabinet. This stage is primarily responsible for transferring the defects of the wall onto the cabinet.

3. **Trim along the scribe lines:** With great care, cut following the scribed lines that are located on the side of the cabinet. You are essentially creating an edge that is tailored to your specifications and conforms to the contours of the wall.

4. **Reposition and secure:** Since your cabinet now has a customized edge, you should place it against the wall and then secure it. Even when placed against the roughest of surfaces, you'll find that it fits snugly and comfortably, just like a glove. After you have scribed your way to an error-free cabinet installation, you can then go ahead and secure it in place.

Scribing Countertops

Lastly, let's explore scribing countertops. Also these elements often encounter walls that aren't perfectly straight or corners that deviate from 90 degrees but of course you want your countertop to fit snugly and seamlessly against these imperfections. Scribing ensures that it does just that.

1. **Position the countertop:** Position the countertop in the position where it will be used, making sure that it is level and that it has adequate support. You will find, much as in the previous examples, that there are spaces between the wall and the countertop.
2. **Scribe the wall's contours:** Using your compass or scribing tool, you should now trace the wall's irregularities onto the edge of your countertop in order to help you position the countertop correctly. After completing this step you will have an edge that is exactly tailored to the contours of the wall.
3. **Trim along the scribe lines:** Carefully cut along the scribed lines on the countertop's edge.
4. **Reposition and secure:** Now you can place the countertop against the wall and then secure it. You are going to be astounded by how perfectly it fits, even up against the most peculiar walls.

Creating reusable templates

Let's say you're making a set of elaborate bespoke cabinets or a series of exquisite chairs that all need the same ornamental scrollwork. There would be discrepancies and extra hours of labor if you were to recreate each element by hand without the help of templates.

The solution lies in the use of reusable templates that are expertly carved guides that ensure flawless replication of intricate designs. To make and use effective reusable templates, consider the following:

1. To begin, select a robust material, such plywood or acrylic, to use as your template. It is expected that this material would retain its shape and durability after extensive use.
2. Design your template: Make a rough drawing of the shape you intend to copy, being sure your design is detailed and accurate in order to perfectly reflect the final product you desire.
3. Cut the template: Carefully remove the pattern from the template material using your cutting tool but be careful and consider that accuracy is essential since any mistakes will show up in the finished product.

4. Smooth the edges: To avoid any imperfections in your routed pieces, sand the edges of your template until they are smooth and free of burrs.

5. Test for accuracy: make sure your template is accurate by practicing on spare wood before attempting it on your actual workpiece. You may then adjust the template to achieve the desired effects.

6. Secure the template: When you're happy with the template's performance, clamp it or use double-sided tape to keep it in place on your workpiece. Take care that it doesn't move when you're routing it.

7. Router magic: Now comes the fun part: with a router fitted with a flush-trim bit to follow the template's contours create a perfect replica of your design.

8. Repeat as needed: Once you have your template set up, you'll find that producing many copies of the same thing is a breeze. To continue routing, you need only move the template to the next piece of wood. Repeat the process as many times as necessary.

Chapter 7: Cutting and Shaping Wood

Mastering Saw Techniques

Quick Overview of Types of Saws for Woodworking.

Before delving into the art of mastering saw techniques, it's crucial to familiarize yourself with the primary types of saws used in woodworking. Each type is designed for specific tasks, so selecting the right saw for the job is a fundamental step.

1. **Handsaws:** These manual saws come in various types, each tailored to specific cutting tasks. Common handsaws include:
   - **Crosscut Saw:** This saw is designed for cutting across the grain of the wood to produce crosscuts that are smooth and clean.
   - **Rip Saw:** This saw is perfect for cutting with the grain of the wood, making it appropriate for ripping as well as rough cuts.
   - **Dovetail Saw**: it is ideal for precise woodworking and work that requires attention to detail since its blade has delicate teeth.
   - **Backsaw:** it is characterized by a reinforced back and is an excellent tool for making accurate and straight cuts in carpentry.
2. **Power Saws:** Electric saws offer efficiency and precision in woodworking. Common power saws include:
   - **Circular Saw:** it is a versatile tool that can do crosscuts, bevel cuts, and straight cuts provided that the appropriate blade is used.
   - **Jigsaw**: it is one of the most useful tools for complex work because of its ability to make precise curved cuts and forms.
   - **Miter Saw:** This saw is great for cutting accurate angles and making miter joints for moldings and frames.
3. **Band Saw:** Featuring a continuous loop of sharp teeth, it's used for curved and irregular cuts, resawing, and intricate designs.

4. **Scroll Saw:** Designed for intricate scrollwork and delicate cuts in thin wood, plywood, and plastic.

How to Select the Appropriate Saw

Now that you have a basic understanding of the types of saws available, let's explore how to select the appropriate tool for your woodworking tasks. Here are some considerations when selecting a saw:

1. Determine the type of cut you need, such as a crosscut, a rip cut, or a specialty cut, and then select a saw that is suitable for making that type of cut.
2. Material: Before beginning, think about the kind of wood you will be working with. When cutting dense hardwoods, you might need a different saw than when cutting plywood or softer woods.
3. Accuracy: If accuracy is of the utmost importance, you should select a saw that is capable of making precise cuts, such as a miter saw for cutting angles or a dovetail saw for cutting joints.
4. adaptability: Certain saws, such as circular saws, offer a high degree of adaptability, allowing for a broad variety of cuts; as a result, these saws are a good choice for novices.
5. Make sure you will be able to securely utilize the saw you have chosen. For instance, using a power saw requires that you take care and wear protective gear.

Proper Hand Placement and Body Posture.

Establish the correct hand placement and body posture before starting sawing is fundamental to ensure both precision and safety:

1. **Hand Placement:** Hold the saw's handle with a firm yet comfortable grip. Place your index finger along the saw's blade for better control over the cut
2. **Stance:** Position yourself so that your feet are shoulder-width apart and perpendicular to the surface you will be working on as this is a solid position that enables greater control of the situation.
3. **Body Alignment:** Make sure that your body is aligned with the cut line at all times. Avoid bending over or reaching too far, since doing either of these things might result in inaccurate results or even accidents.

4. **Eye Protection:** When working with wood or sawdust, you should always use safety goggles to protect your eyes from sawdust and wood particles.

Creating Straight Cuts

Keep in mind that the ability to make straight cuts is one that may be honed with practice. Do not let the early mistakes you make discourage you; they are all a necessary part of the learning experience. When you make a cut, look at it as a chance to improve your technique and go one step closer to being a woodworking expert.

When it comes to straight cuts, here's how to harness the power of hand saws.

1. **Choose the Right Hand Saw:** There are several varieties of hand saws, each one optimized for a certain kind of cutting. Your best bet for making cuts in a straight line is either a crosscut saw or a rip saw. Rip saws are intended for cutting with the grain of the wood, whereas crosscut saws contain fine teeth that are meant for cutting across the grain.

2. **Mark Your Cut:** Before You Start Sawing You should use a pencil or knife to mark your intended cut line before you start sawing. Throughout the cut, this mark will act as your compass and guide you in the right direction.

3. **Stabilize the Workpiece:** You can use clamps or a vise to securely secure the workpiece that you are working on. Cutting in a straight line and reducing the likelihood of injury both depend on a workpiece that is stable.

4. **Start with a Starter Groove:** Create a thin starter groove that runs parallel to your cut line; this will create a path that your saw may follow, lowering the likelihood that it will veer off in an unexpected direction.

5. **Practice Patience:** Before you start sawing, ensure that the rhythm you are using is uniform and consistent. Avoid moving too quickly through the cut and instead let the teeth of the saw do the work. Use a little but constant amount of pressure.

6. **Stay Aligned:** Make sure the saw blade is aligned with the line you want to cut, in fact it is impossible to make a straight cut without this alignment being correct. Keep in mind that there is no turning back once you have strayed from the path!

7. **Use a Guide:** When making longer cuts, you should seriously consider making use of a straightedge or a wooden guide to assist in keeping the saw on the correct path. This is something that may be extremely helpful for novices.

Now, let's explore how to achieve straight cuts with power saws.

1. **Select the Right Power Saw:** You have the option of using either a circular saw, a miter saw, or a jigsaw depending on the project that you are working on. Miter saws are excellent at making exact cuts at angles, while circular saws are more adaptable and work well for making straight cuts.

2. **Set the Depth:** You will need to adjust the cutting depth of your power saw so that it is appropriate for the thickness of the material you are cutting; this guarantees a clean and thorough cut without causing any damage to the surface that lies beneath.

3. **Secure Your Workpiece:** is just as important when using power saws as it is when using hand saws. Make use of some clamps or a workbench.

4. **Align the Blade:** Place the saw's blade in such a position that it perfectly aligns with the cut line you have drawn. The majority of electric saws are equipped with either guides or laser markers to assist users in achieving precision.

5. **Smooth Start:** Before turning on the saw, make sure the blade is not in contact with the workpiece. Then, slowly bring the blade down onto the wood. This eliminates the possibility of any abrupt jolts or movements that might result in uneven cutting.

6. **Keep Control:** As you move the saw down the cut line, make sure you keep a strong grip on the saw and on the cutting tool. Keep a steady pace and avoid pushing the saw through the wood by using undue power

7. **Safety First:** Put on safety eyewear and hearing protection, and make sure you follow the instructions provided by the manufacturer.

Tips for Maintaining a Straight Cutting Line

Creating straight cuts isn't just about the tools; it's also about the techniques. Here are some valuable tips to keep in mind:

1. **Stay Calm and Focused:** Woodworking requires patience and concentration. T Take your time, concentrate on making the incision, and stay away from anything that may distract you.

2. **Practice on Scrap Wood:** If you are new to woodworking or are attempting a new method, you should first become experienced dealing with scrap wood as it is a wonderful opportunity to hone your abilities without the stress of having to produce a final product.

3. **Measure Twice, Cut Once:** I have already told you this marvelous age-old adage... Double-check your measurements and cut lines before making the cut to avoid costly mistakes.

4. **Maintain Sharp Blades:** Rough cuts and splintering can be caused by blades that have lost their sharpness. Maintaining your saw blades by sharpening or replacing them on a regular basis can ensure clean cuts.

5. **Consider a Zero-Clearance Insert:** Using a power saw that has a zero-clearance insert will help reduce the amount of tear-out and ensure a cleaner cut.

6. **Use a Straightedge:** Whether you're working with a circular saw or a jigsaw, a straightedge guide may be a game-changer for keeping your cuts straight across a greater distance.

7. **Embrace Hand Planes:** After you have made your cuts, you may further polish and straighten edges by using hand planes because these tools make it possible to make fine adjustments and smooth things out.

Curved and Angled Cuts

When dealing with wood, making curved cuts can be both a challenge and a gratifying experience. It is similar to the craft of sculpting, in which extra wood is removed by chiselling in order to expose the hidden beauty that is contained inside. Here's how to do it:

1. **Plan Your Curve:** Before you begin cutting away at your workpiece, you should first draw out the curve that you want it to have. It's similar to drawing out a map of your route before you set out on the road.

2. **Cut Outside the Line** Before you begin sawing, you should set your sights on cutting just outside the line that has been drawn. You'll leave yourself some wiggle space for fine-tuning and smoothing out later if you do it this way.

3. **Use a Jigsaw or Bandsaw:** Create sweeping curves with the help of a jigsaw or bandsaw, which are your greatest friends when it comes to working with saws. Because of their mobility, traversing complicated shapes is not a difficult task.

4. **Maintain a Slow and Steady Pace:** In contrast to straight cuts, curved cuts require a more delicate touch. It's all about precision, so take it slow, keep your eyes on the line, and don't lose your temper.

5. **Sandpaper is Your Best Friend:** After you've finished making the first cut, it's time to use sandpaper to polish the curves you just formed. Obtaining a finish that is as smooth as silk requires the use of a decent sanding block.

6. **Practice Makes Perfect:** Curved cuts might be tough at first, so don't let first glitches discourage you from practicing more. Practice makes perfect. Practice is the only way to become an expert in anything related to woodworking.

Achieving Precise Miter Cuts

With miter cuts it's all about angles, and nailing them down can really take your woodworking projects to the next level. Imagine them as the chic joints that are responsible for bringing the corners together in a smooth manner. Miter cuts might be difficult to master but here are some helpful hints:

1. **Choose Your Weapon** Miter cuts may be accomplished using a variety of saws, including miter saws, table saws, and even hand saws for those who are looking for a challenge.

2. **Measure and Mark:** Miter cuts require a high level of precision. Take precise readings of your angle measurements, then mark them on your workpiece. There is no space for speculation here.

3. **Become Skilled in the process** When cutting miter joints, it is not enough to simply have the right equipment; you also need to be skilled in the process. Cut carefully and steadily while ensuring that your saw blade remains aligned with the angle that you have marked.

4. **Test the fit:** After you have completed your miter cuts, you should perform a dry-fit test to determine how well the pieces match with one another. It's possible that some adjustments are going to be required for the perfect, gap-free fit.

5. **add Glue to the Mitered Surfaces and Join Them Together** Once you are pleased with the way the pieces fit together, add glue to the mitered surfaces and join the pieces together. During the time that the glue has to dry, you can use clamps or tape to assist hold everything in place.

6. **smooth the Finish:** Once the glue has dried, you may use sandpaper or a block plane to smooth the edges of the mitered joints. The objective is to establish a link that is unbroken and unbrokenly smooth.

7. **Practice makes perfect:** just as with any other woodworking skill, learning miter cuts requires a lot of repetition and refinement. And the more practice you put in with angles, the more proficient you'll become with them.

The Jigsaw Puzzle

It's easy enough to make circular or curved cuts, but what about designs that call for straight ones? The jigsaw zips across these surfaces with little trouble at all.

If you want to make a complex pattern or a curve of any kind (circles, arcs, or ellipses), this is the tool for you. The jigsaw is versatile, allowing you to cut through wood, plastic, metal, and even ceramics and it may serve as a reliable companion in a variety of contexts. It is a lightweight and manageable alternative to heavier power instruments. I'm sure that both novice and expert woodworkers will find this to be an invaluable resource.

Want to replicate a specific design or shape? Attach a template or pattern to your workpiece and let the jigsaw follow the lines. Ever wondered how to create those internal cutouts in a piece of wood? The jigsaw can plunge right in and carve out your desired shape.

Thanks to its narrow blade profile, it can access tight corners and spots that other saws might struggle with.

Blade types must vary depending on the substance being cut. Teeth per inch (TPI) is also important, with higher TPI allowing for cleaner cuts and lower TPI allowing for faster cutting.

Blades come in various tooth configurations such as up-cut, down-cut, and bi-metal. If you want the best outcomes, you should think about the teeth's cutting orientation: a longer blade may make a broader cut, while a shorter one is easier to wield precisely. Select a time frame that works for your project. Of course Jigsaw blades wear out much like any other cutting tool, so it's important to always have fresh, sharp blades on hand.

Mastering the jigsaw takes practice. It's like solving a puzzle – each project is a new challenge, a new adventure. Embrace the versatility, experiment with blade types, and marvel at the intricate shapes you can achieve.

Crosscuts vs. Rip Cuts

At this point, it is important to clarify the difference between crosscuts and rip cuts. It's a bit like distinguishing between a left turn and a right turn: in fact they take you in different directions (but both are essential skills).

Crosscuts – The All-Angle Slicers: Think of crosscuts as the maestros of angular slices. Crosscutting is done when a board is sliced across its width or at an angle. These cuts are like the spice of woodworking, adding flavor and dimension to your projects.

Rip Cuts – The Lengthwise Dividers: Rip Cuts In contrast, rip cuts prioritize length. Rip cutting is used when you need to divide a board lengthwise to get thinner strips. These cuts are like the building blocks of your projects, laying the foundation for your designs.

Efficient Methods for Common Cuts

Now that we've got our terminology straight, let's explore some efficient methods for these common cuts. Imagine you're crafting a wooden masterpiece – these techniques are your trusty brushes, ready to bring your vision to life.

Crosscut Capers: When it comes to crosscuts, precision is key. Here's how to slice and dice like a pro:

- *Square It Up:* Make sure the edge of your workpiece is square before proceeding, it's like having a solid launchpad for your rocket.
- *Mark the Spot:* Make sure your cut line is precise by using a square as a measuring tool. Keep in mind that a skewed line will result in an uneven slice.

- *Stay on the Line:* Follow the designated line closely (it is your blueprint for success) whether you're using a handsaw or a power saw.
- *Safety First:* Safety must always come first so put on safety gear, keep your hands off the knife, and go slow and steady.

Rip cuts may seem straightforward, but there's an art to achieving clean, straight lines:
- Find Your Line: Similar to crosscuts, marking your cut line is essential, in fact precision begins with a clear path.
- Set the Fence: If you're using a table saw, set the rip fence to the desired width. It's like setting the stage for your cut.
- Go Against the Grain: Splintering is common with rip cuts because they are made perpendicular to the grain of the wood. Tear-out may be avoided by maintaining a sharp blade and cutting slowly and steadily.

Some tips

First of all remember that your choice of blade matters. For crosscuts, opt for a blade with more teeth for smoother finishes; rip cuts thrive with blades featuring fewer teeth, allowing for efficient material removal.

When dealing with rip cuts on power saws, use push sticks and featherboards to keep your hands safe and maintain control. It's like having extra hands to guide the way.

Ensure proper support for your workpiece throughout the cut as an unsteady piece can lead to uneven results.

Don't' worry if your first few cuts might resemble a Picasso rather than a Michelangelo, that's all part of the journey. Don't shy away from experimentation, and embrace the occasional mishap as a learning opportunity!

In woodworking, routing involves rapid cutting, trimming, and shaping woodworking materials to apply in a particular woodwork project for a perfect look. Here, the woodworker uses a router, a tool you can mount on the table or hold by hand as you do the process.

If you are a beginner, you must take precautions since the routing process can be dangerous, especially if you don't know how to operate the tool. However, you can always refer to the manufacturer's instructions when doubting.

Since the routers have different bits installed in them, you can use them to perform different tasks and create stunning decorative work.

- Trimming and edging are two of the many tasks that routers excel at. For example you could add a decorative edge to a tabletop or smooth off rough edges on a cabinet
- Creating elaborate joinery such as dovetail joints or other complex joinery? Routers are the key ingredient in this dish.

- Do you need to fashion your wooden masterpiece with a variety of delicate hollows or grooves? Thanks to the router you will be able to scoop out wood with precision, so your projects will have more depth and personality.
- Smoothing uneven patterns after using glue.
- Creating a hole in the center of the project.
- Making an even circle.
- Making the same and even patterns.
- Cutting dadoes to build shelves.
- Making frame and panel cabinet doors.

Types of Routers

Routers may come in various sizes and they may have different names, but they typically fit into one of these categories:

- Trim routers—These are tiny routers that may often be handled with one hand. Sometimes they are termed palm routers or hand routers. Trim routers normally feature ¼" collets for ¼" router bit shanks and are best suited for little details like adding ornamental edges.

- Plunge routers—These have a "springy looking base" that enables you to plunge the bit into the wood and bring it back up. This is handy for carving signs when you need to elevate the piece between letters or graphics you are carving.

- Fixed base routers—Fixed base routers are routers that constantly cut at the same depth. Now, the depth is changeable between cuts, but unlike a plunge router, you can't raise and plunge while it's cutting—hence the phrase "fixed base." They generally have two handles on each side so they may be grasped and operated with two hands. And they are generally bigger and more powerful than trim routers. They may come in dozens of sizes and might be ¼" or ½" collets.

Note: A collet is the metal sleeve of a router that you slide a router bit into. A shank is the component of a router bit that is placed into the router.

Rounding Edges and Creating Profiles

Let's take a closer look at the skill of rounding edges and crafting profiles. Whether you're working on a simple shelf or an intricate piece of furniture, these router techniques add a professional touch.

Have you ever scraped your skin on the corner of a sharply-edged piece of furniture? Ouch! Safety and irony aside, your project will seem much more professional with those sharp corners rounded off. Choosing the appropriate router bit is the trick to successfully rounding off corners, in fact there are precise bits designed to smooth over or shape edges that works wonderfully for this purpose. Then you have to adjust the depth of the router in order to create the curve you want: for a softer, rounder finish, begin with a shallower setting and work your way up. Always wear safety goggles, ear protection and a dust mask when using a router. Safety should be always your top priority.

The purpose of a profile is all about giving your project character and depth, and here you can let your creativity shines, whether it's a decorative edge on a tabletop or a unique trim on a cabinet.

*Also in this case you have first to select the Right Bit, as d*ifferent router bits create various profiles. Be sure to choose a bit that matches your design vision. Start practicing on a scrap piece of wood before diving into your project in order to get comfortable with the router's movement and the desired profile. Working against the wood grain helps reduce tear-out while cutting profiles. However, going against the grain isn't always the best option. Find out what works best for your design by trying different things.

Remember that, when routing profiles, a stable workpiece is essential (clamps or a router table can help you keep your work under control and ensure safety)

Just to give you an example of practical application, when I was crafting a set of custom shelves for my home, I decided to add a decorative edge using a router. I chose a Roman ogee bit for a classic look. It was my first time attempting a decorative edge and hoenstly I was a bit nervous. After practicing on a scrap piece of wood, I felt more confident and went to work on the actual shelves. The results were astounding! The decorative edges added a touch of elegance to my shelves, and I couldn't have been happier.

Exploring Wood Planers

Planing is a fundamental woodworking process that smooths out the wood and removes unnecessary pieces that can otherwise make the wood difficult to work with; a planer is usually used after a jointer has smoothed out the first face of the lumber. Moreover with the use of wood planers, you can ensure that your product has a uniform thickness throughout. When it comes to making worktops, cabinets, or even complex inlays, maintaining a consistent thickness is essential for both the appearance and the functioning of the final product.

Do you want to construct your very own bespoke moldings to give your project that special touch? Planers have also the capability of being fitted with molding knives, which enables users to create their own custom profiles.

Depending on the process and result, you might choose to use a hand planer or an electric planer: the first ones are good if you are working with small pieces of wood and need to get some detailed work done, while the others are used to remove different uneven pieces from larger pieces of wood. If you are working with a small amount of lumber and you want to create less dust, it is best to opt for a hand planer. If you are working with a lot of wood and need to complete your project efficiently, opt for an electric planer.

As with other woodworking tools, there are different planes for different needs. The most common type of plane is the bench plane, which is used to plane out uneven lumber. The most common type of bench plane is the jack plane, used to smooth out the surface of an entire piece of lumber. You can also use a trying plane, but it is larger than other planes. You can also use a block planes (these are made of metal and have some unique characteristics) but they are for smaller pieces that require more precision and detail.

I remember the first time I used a power planer: The ease with which it smoothed down uneven surfaces and changed rough timber into a flawlessly flat one astounded me!

In addition to choosing the right type of plane for the job, make sure that you sharpen it before you use it, even if you are working with a new plane. While using the plane, adjust the angle of the blade to control the thickness of the shavings and to get the even surface you desire.

Power planers often come equipped with a thickness adjustment capability that makes it easy to achieve the desired result (in terms of thickness) at any given setting.

Remember that grain direction is important: always plane in the direction of the grain to prevent tear-out. When you plane against the grain of the wood, you run the risk of creating unattractive gouges and splintering.

Mastering Chisels and Gouges

You need to gather all of your chisels and gouges before beginning your masterpiece in woodworking so that you can have a good start. Imagine that you are selecting the appropriate paintbrushes to go with your canvas. Chisels and gouges come in a variety of forms and sizes, each of which is designed for a particular job, from making straight cuts to detailed carving.

Keeping chisels and gouges in a state of razor-sharpness is the single most important step in getting the most out of their use, in fact as you can easily imagine trying to carve or shape material with a dull chisel or gouge is analogous to painting with a crusty, dried-out brush. It is necessary to hone your tools with the same attention that a samurai would put into sharpening their sword. Once again I want to stress that safety should be your primary concern whenever you are dealing with wood, regardless of the project at hand, and chisels and gouges are dangerous tools that can cause injury if they are not handled with respect. Always make sure you're using protective gear and try to keep your work area as clean as possible.

Shaping, Carving, and Detailing Techniques

Step 1: Plan Your Design

Have a crystal clear concept of the design you want to create before you even think about picking up any tools. You may do the sketch on paper or, if you're feeling confident, you can do it right on the wood. If you have a plan, it will be easier for you to remain on track and prevent you from overcarving.

Step 3: Secure Your Workpiece

To ensure both accuracy and safety while working, you can use clamps or a vice to securely hold your workpiece in place, preventing any unwanted movement during the carving process.

Step 4: Make Guiding Marks

Make guide markings with a pencil or a marking knife if the design you're working on demands certain proportions or symmetrical patterns. This will help you get the design exactly how you want it. These markers serve as points of reference and contribute to the preservation of symmetry.

Step 5: Begin with Shallow Cuts

Start with shallow cuts: there is always time to remove more wood if needed, but you can't put it back once it's gone! Begin carving by tapping the chisel or gouge gently with a mallet taking your time to get a feel for the tool's action.

Step 6: Follow Your Design

Carefully follow your design, working from the general shape to the finer details. Keep in mind that carving is a subtractive process that means that you are working to unveil the finished item by eliminating material.

Step 7: Vary Techniques

It's possible that you'll need to use a variety of different methods, depending on the design you choose; for instance, a gouge is useful for efficiently removing big sections of wood, while a chisel is more suited for working on finer details. Experiment with various gouge shapes to arrive at the desired textures for your project.

Step 8: Maintain Sharpness

Sharp tools are crucial for clean and controlled cuts Take breaks at regular intervals to sharpen your chisels and gouges as the use of dull instruments can increase the risk of accidents and poor results.

Step 9: Pay Attention to Grain Direction

Carving relies heavily on following the natural grain of the wood. As you work, be aware of the direction in which the grain runs and keep in mind the following advices: carve along the grain for smoother cuts, and carve against the grain for more detailed contouring and sculpting.

Step 10: Test and Adjust

Take a step back at regular intervals and evaluate your development. Examine how well your work adheres to the design, and make any required changes.

Step 11: Refine and Finish

After you have carved the primary design, you should shift your attention to perfecting the details, for example you could decide to create more delicate details, use chisels and gouges with finer blades. Now you can sand the area that was cut so that there are no tool marks left behind and the finish is smooth.

Molding

Molding is a process of creating and shaping wood for decorative profiles and transitions between different surfaces; it allows craftsmen to express the art of intricate woodwork through the pieces they create.

There are several methods you can consider:

- Router Magic: Utilizing a router that has been fitted with a number of different profile bits is one of the most flexible ways. Imagine it as a chisel that a sculptor would use, only for wood. Using the router, you may quickly and easily change straight edges into stunning curves, ogees, coves, or any other profile that your heart wants.

- Carving Wonders: Carving is the key to unlocking your own talent, as it allows you to construct intricate molding designs; it's like drawing on wood, only with more precise instruments.
- Turning Perfect Cylindrical Moldings on a Lathe. That's perfect if you're in love with symmetry...you should attempt turning perfect cylindrical moldings on a lathe to use as table legs or ornamental spindles. It's like doing ballet with your chisels and gouges!
- Stock and Bond: The application of pre-made trim pieces is all that is required for some types of moldings. Simply go to the store, get a design that appeals to you, and secure it to the wall with a dab of glue or some discrete nails. Adding this to your project is similar to accessorizing it with a chic piece.

As an art that has changed over time, there are different types of molding. Astragal is a type of molding that has been used for ages and is even found in modern homes because it is both decorative and functional. It is a semicircular type of molding that covers the gaps between two door parts where they meet.

Convex molding is a type of molding created in the shape of rope; this is a Romanesque style of molding that you can see in many Western European buildings in countries such as England, France, and Spain. It was particularly famous during the 18th century. Casing is an intricate, decorative border molding that you might see around doors and window panes; this type of molding is used to bridge the gap between the door parts and the surrounding wall to create one seamless, solid design. Casing is still popular and can be seen in many modern homes.

Crown molding is another type of molding that began in earlier eras but remains popular today, and it is used to decorate the lines where ceilings meet walls or to highlight points of wall lighting.

Molding adds to the beauty and detailing of a home and furniture, as it conceals joints that might otherwise look plain and grotesque. In doing so, it increases the value of both property and furniture.

Chapter 8: Joinery techniques

Joinery isn't just a technique, it is the backbone of woodworking itself. It's the invisible force that ensures your creations are more than mere assemblies of wood, but durable, stable, and lasting pieces of functional art. It isn't a one-size-fits-all endeavor; it's a rich tapestry of techniques, each with its unique purpose and charm.

In this chapter, we will introduce the main ways you can create joints, as well as the different types of joints and their characteristics.

Pocket-hole joint

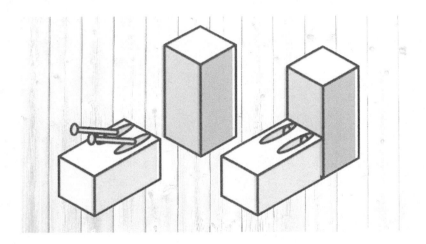

A pocket-hole joint is commonly used in woodworking because it is versatile and easy to make. Basically, it involves drilling an angled hole into one piece of wood and attaching it to another piece with screws. To drill the hole at the correct angle, consider around 15 degrees

When joining the two pieces, you need to use a self-drilling washer head screw; a drill and a pocket hold jig will also be helpful. First, measure and mark the locations where you'll drill the pocket holes, then position the pocket-hole jig so that the marked drilling locations align with the jig's guide holes. Now you can proceed inserting the drill bit into the jig's guide hole. If possible, use clamps to secure the wood pieces you're joining to a stable surface in order to prevent them from moving during drilling.

And you are ready to assemble the joint:

- If you used clamps, you should remove them once you have finished drilling the pocket holes.
- Along the edge of one of the pieces of wood that are going to be linked together, apply a little amount of wood glue. This step isn't always required, but doing it can provide the joint a little bit more support when it's needed.
- Align the two pieces of wood so that the pocket hole and the pilot hole are aligned properly with one another.
- Using a screwdriver or a drill equipped with a screwdriver bit and a second piece of wood, drive pocket-hole screws through the holes and into the second piece of wood. It is important not to overtighten the screws since doing so might cause the wood to crack.

From large furniture to small picture frames, pocket joints come in handy in many situations. They can be visible, but you can fix that by filling the drilled holes.

Biscuit joint

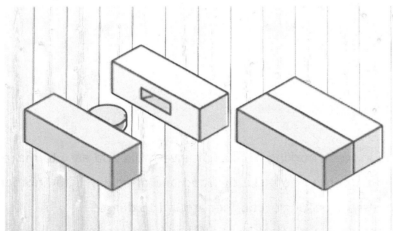

Biscuit joints are also very common in woodworking and are used to connect different wood types without using screws or nails.

To create a biscuit joint, you have to use a biscuit joiner (also known as a plate joiner), which is a handy tool with a circular blade that enables you to cut the so-called "biscuit slots" (half-oval-shaped slots) into the 2 pieces of wood that you are joining. Now, you can insert the biscuit—not the edible one! It is a special oval piece of compressed wood that you can buy at any specialized store.

Prior to inserting the biscuit, fill the slots with glue. Then, when the slot biscuit goes in, it expands and fits perfectly. This creates great joints without the use of any other tools or fixtures like nails, and once you've had practice, they are easy to make. Although they're not very strong, they do provide a seamless finish and are great for cabinets and bookshelves.

Tongue and groove joint

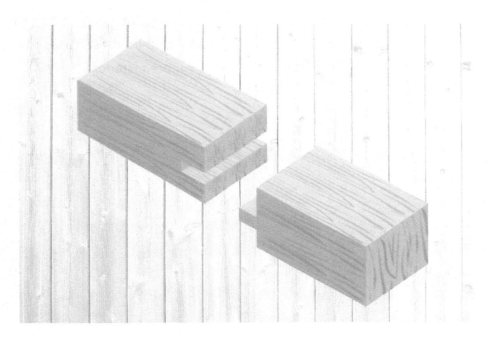

Anyone who has ever laid wood or laminate flooring will be familiar with tongue and groove joints. This is the type of joint that is used to join two flat objects from edge to edge. The tongue from one piece extends out toward the socket of the other piece and fits into the socket to secure the joint. These joints are created by butting the edge of the two flat objects together and using a fastener to make a joint. Tongue and groove joints are strong and are used to hold multiple surfaces because they have a large adjoining surface area.

1. Craft "the tongue". You may sculpt the projecting ridge that runs along one side of the first board by using a table saw or a router. The end result should be a tongue that is accurate and rectangular.

2. Now carve a matching groove along the edge of the second board. This can be done using a router, dado set, or a specialized tongue and groove bit. The groove should be just wide and deep enough to accommodate the tongue.

3. The grand union. Slide the tongue into the welcoming slot. When they are brought closer together, there is typically a quiet but gratifying "click" that may be heard as the parts lock into place.

4. Sealing the deal. Before putting the boards together, many skilled woodworkers add wood glue in order to ensure that the resulting union will be even more successful. Once the two pieces have been joined together, the connection can be further strengthened by adding screws or nails, but in most cases the connection is already robust enough to not require any more fasteners.

Mortise and tenon joint

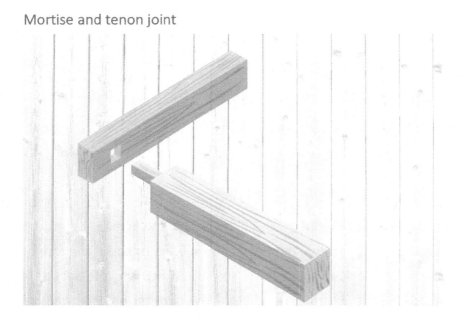

The mortise and tenon joint is another common wood joint. The mortise is the pocket cut that is made into the wood, and the tenon is the corresponding protruding part of another piece of wood that fits into the pocket cut to form the joint (this is usually done by trimming or sawing

84

one end of the first piece of wood). You can carve out the mortise using a chisel, router, or mortising machine. It's essential to ensure the mortise is accurately sized and aligned with the tenon for a perfect fit.

The mortise is usually cut at an angle of 90 degrees, and the tenon is set up at an angle to match the mortise, which provides the joint's strength and durability. This formation keeps the joint from ripping out or moving out of square. Also in this case, woodworkers often introduce a bit of wood glue into the mortise before joining the pieces in order to make their union even more robust.

There are many variations on the mortise and tenon joint: it can be found in rectangular and square forms, as well as pinned and wedged forms. Commercially available tools, such as a table saw, can be used to create the mortises and tenons for this type of joint.

Bridle joint

The bridle joint is fairly and similar to the mortise and tenon joint and it is usually good for large joining work. At its heart, the bridle joint is all about joining two pieces of wood at a right angle: the two boards are joined together by an elaborate overlap that is created by one board extending into the other. It resembles a horse's bridle, hence the name.

The notching of one of the boards is the first stage in the process of making a bridle joint. This groove is often formed in the shape of a rectangle or a square and is created with the use of tools like saws, chisels, or routers. This part, which has a notch cut out of it, is where the second board will fit. On the second piece there will be a protruding section, often in the shape of a rectangle or a square so that it may fit snuggly into the groove that is already present in the initial board.

Dovetail joint

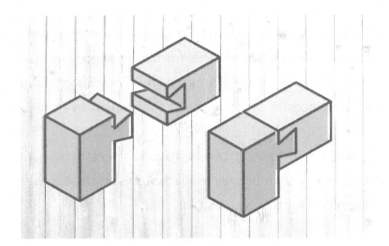

Dovetail joints are frequently found in furniture. They use pins and tails, which fit together to form joints that cannot be pulled apart. When done properly, it creates a sequence of trapezoidal pins (or tails) on one piece of wood that interlock with comparable tails (or pins) on the other. This produces a distinctive, fan-like design, which is frequently evident on the edges of drawers and boxes. It's more than simply a joint; it's a piece of art.

It is very strong, but it is not easy to create and set up. You can create it with a saw and chisel, but you must ensure that the pins and tails are well aligned. You can also use router templates to make the layout and alignment perfect, which is absolutely necessary for dovetail joints to work properly.

Dovetail joints come in a variety of styles, each with its own set of characteristics:

- Through Dovetail: Because this connection is visible from both sides of the wood, it is ideal for projects where aesthetics are important on both the inside and outside, such as drawers.
- Half-Blind Dovetail: This joint covers the end grain of the opposite side, providing a cleaner, more completed appearance. It is frequently utilized in high-end cabinets.
- Sliding Dovetail: A long, sliding tail that fits into a matching groove, giving strength to lengthy joints.

Box joint

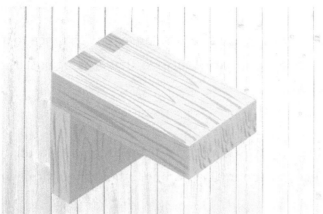

A box joint, also known as a finger joint, is another type of joint that wood workers should know about. It is created using an interweaving technique that makes it resemble two hands with interwoven fingers (hence, finger joint). A box joint is a very clean joint that works well for different kinds of furniture. Box joints can be used in place of dovetail joints, and they are less expensive and less difficult to create.

Firstly, you have to measure and mark. Both parts should have the length of the joint measured and marked on them. The number of fingers or slots that may be created is directly proportional to the length of the joint. Make sure that the joints on both pieces are aligned before you mark the places for the fingers. Mark the positions uniformly throughout the width of the board.

Now it's time to gather your tools and you have basically 2 choices: either use a table saw equipped with a dado blade or a router table in conjunction with a matching router bit.

You are ready to cut the "fingers":
- For a table saw:
  Attach a dado stack to the table of your table saw, and then adjust its height so that it corresponds to the desired depth of the fingers. Install a miter gauge that has an extension fence, and then set it so that it aligns with the markings you made. In order to make the fingers, you will need to carefully pass your workpiece through the dado stack, being sure to stop exactly at each designated location.

- For a router table: Install a router bit that matches, and then adjust the height of the bit so that it matches the depth of the fingers.

  You may equip your router table with a miter gauge by attaching an extension fence to it. You may construct the fingers by positioning your workpiece so that it is against the fence, and then moving it over the router bit.

After obtaining slots with squared ends, remove the waste material from them with a utility knife, apply a little bit of glue, and slide the pieces together. Use clamps to hold them firmly in place.

Butt joint

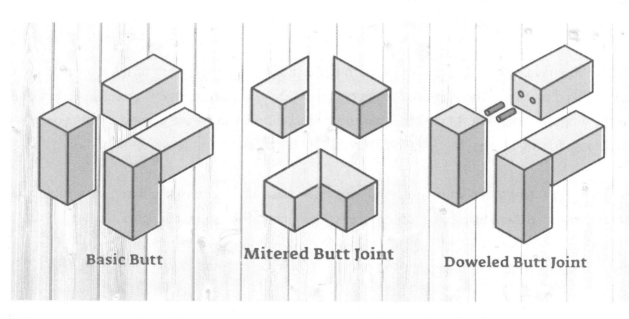

Basic Butt   **Mitered Butt Joint**   **Doweled Butt Joint**

A butt joint is a simple joint that forms when the end grain bumps directly up to the long grain face at 90 degrees. The butt joint is easy to execute and does not require as much work as other types of joint. Although a butt joint is easy to use and create, it needs to be reinforced and created well for it to be strong. It is commonly used for simple woodworking tasks such as constructing basic frames, attaching back panels to cabinets, or building temporary structures.

88

It should be doweled or screwed for extra fastening and strength. Moreover, there is a risk of the board swelling due to moisture, which weakens the joint over time. A basic butt joint is created when two pieces of wood butt into each other edgewise. Most often, it creates a right angle between the two pieces of wood. They are common for creating frames like door or window frames. A mitered butt joint is similar to a basic butt joint, but it has an advantage in that it does not show an end grain. A mitered joint is often preferred because it has a more attractive appearance. However, it's is not as strong as other joints.

Half lap joint

A half lap joint is easy to make, requiring only two cuts and the chisel to clean it up before joining. Although it is not that strong, it is a good joint for glue application because it has good glue surfaces on both edges. If the glue used for fastening is good, the effect and strength is also good. In any case it is stronger than a butt joint. It involves removing material from two adjoining pieces of wood so that they overlap each other by half of their thickness; this creates a flush and secure connection between the two pieces. They are commonly used in woodworking for a variety of applications, including building frames, shelves, and cabinets.

First, you'll need to measure and mark the thickness of the wood pieces you'll be joining. Make a note on both parts at the spot where you'll be joining them; then start cutting the half-lap by gently removing the designated material from each piece of wood using a saw (table saw, circular saw, or handsaw). The success of the joint rests on your ability to make straight, precise cuts.

After you've finished making the half-lap cuts, you should try putting the two parts back together to see how well they fit. There shouldn't be any gaps between the two pieces since the cut surfaces didn't line up properly. If the joint isn't a perfect fit, sand it or cut it down till it is.

Apply woodworking glue to the areas where the two pieces of wood will meet, and then assemble them, holding the parts together using a clamp until the glue has dried.

Rabbet Joint

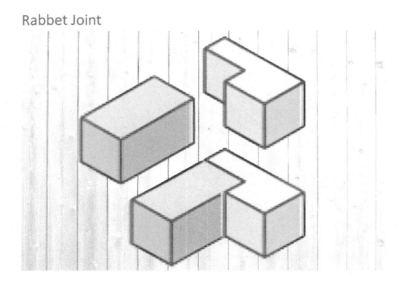

A rabbet joint, also known as a rebate joint, is a common woodworking joint used in cabinetmaking, picture framing, and other woodworking projects where a clean, hidden joint is desired, that involves removing a portion of the edge or end of one piece of wood to create a recess, or "rabbet," into which another piece of wood can fit snugly. This type of joint is often used to join two pieces of wood at a right angle, forming a strong and stable connection.

A always, the first step is to measure and mark the parts where you intend to cut the rabbet.

Then you can start cutting the Rabbet, which can be done with a saw or a router fitted with the proper bit, just make sure your cuts are straight and accurate since they will affect how well the joint fits together. Once the rabbet has been cut, the second piece of wood must be tested to determine if it fits into the newly created cavity. There should be no play, just a snug and solid fit.

90

Apply woodworking glue to the intersecting surfaces of the two wood pieces, then assemble them. Make sure the adhesive holds by clamping the parts together while they dry.

Screws or nails can be used to strengthen the rabbet junction for increased strength, but this step is optional and will depend on the application and joint size.

Gluing and clamping

Gluing is a very common woodworking technique for joining two pieces of wood together. Prior to gluing, the wood must be prepared properly. There are different types of glue that you can work with. For example, white and yellow glue are used for joining, but they are not water resistant. Therefore, these glues are appropriate for use interior the joints but not exterior. However, there is an exterior glue that is water resistant and appropriate for exterior joints or projects that will live outside. Other types of glue include epoxy, which is used to fill gaps and strengthen a structure, and polyurethane glues, which are moisture-activated and bond into a resilient adhesive. PVA glue is the most common wood glue, as it penetrates the wood fibers and creates strong bonds.

Remember to apply it always to both surfaces that are to be bonded, there should be no spills or overflow, and you should use a clean wipe to wipe away any excess. First, spread out the glue into thin, even layers with the help of a brush and spreader; then, put the two pieces together and press. You can also shift the pieces back and forth so that the glue is spread evenly and there are no air bubbles. Use a G clamp to keep the two freshly glued pieces together and leave them undisturbed for the recommended time. Remove any dried excess glue with sandpaper. As you can see, gluing is a fairly easy technique, but you have to be patient and let the wood and glue do the work.

Clamping is another technique for joining two types of wood. Different types of clamps are used for this purpose. Bar clamps and pipe clamps hold together large pieces for joining, while the other clamps, such as F clamps, work well on narrow, small projects. Bar clamps come with a long bar and a jaw that clamps material together; they can be adjusted easily to hold different materials together. Pipe clamps are similar to bar clamps and are used to hold doors and other large pieces of wood together; they are preferred by many people because they can be adjusted by simply altering the length of the pipe between the jaws. This is an easy process that makes pipe clamps very versatile. F clamps are used to hold narrow material or edges together; they can also work as a vise to hold your project down on the work bench to achieve greater stability. Spring-loaded clamps (lightweight and easy to use) are also good for holding projects stable, but these small clamps usually work best for small, narrow projects that are no more than 3 inches wide. Spring-loaded clamps are

Ultimately, every woodworker should have at least some spring-loaded clamps, bar clamps, and pipe clamps in his tool box. When using clamps to secure things, always wear safety goggles to protect your eyes. To choose the right clamps for the job, you need to know the dimensions and nature of wood that you're working with. You also need to consider the weight and strength of the clamp to determine its suitability for holding together wood of different widths and thicknesses. Never choose a clamp that looks out of shape, is bent, or has a broken spindle. Do not use extra-large clamps if you don't need to. When fastening your clamps make sure that the pressure plates and the anvil of the clamp are in contact with the material's surface for a proper fastening effect. Close the jaws tightly so that the clamp holds together properly. Finally, it is important to keep your clamps clean and lightly oiled so that they will store well and be easy to use.

Unleash Your Creativity

Creative joinery is a world where I've discovered endless possibilities during my own woodworking journey.

Decorative joinery is the secret handshake of seasoned woodworkers. When aesthetics and practicality come together in this way, woodworking is elevated to the level of art. To begin incorporating decorative joinery into your project, start by drawing your pattern on the surface of the wood. To create the design you want, first carefully chisel or carve it out, and then carefully fit the ornamental parts into position so that the finish is flat and uninterrupted.

Dovetail Splendor

In addition to their legendary durability, dovetail joints provide a wonderful opportunity for artistic expression. Adding class to your work is as simple as changing the angle and spacing, but you could also get more creative and try out new dovetail patterns like the eye-catching houndstooth or the elegant fan.

- The houndstooth pattern is a distinctive and classic decorative pattern often seen in textiles, fashion, and sometimes in woodworking and other crafts. It typically consists of a repeated geometric design of small, abstract, four-pointed shapes, resembling a checkered pattern. In woodworking, the houndstooth pattern can be created by carefully arranging wood pieces with alternating colors or grain orientations to achieve this visually appealing design. It's a technique that requires precision and attention to detail to achieve the desired effect.

- The fan pattern is a decorative woodworking technique used to create intricate and visually striking designs. This pattern, characterized by elegance and attention to detail, resembles a fan, with the individual "blades" of the fan radiating outward in a symmetrical and artistic manner. To create an elegant fan pattern, woodworkers carefully shape and join individual wood elements, such as strips or veneers, into the desired fan shape. (Moreover these elements are often curved or tapered to create the flowing and graceful appearance of a fan). It can be used to embellish various woodworking projects such as furniture, cabinetry and doors.

The Elegance of Inlays

Inlays are like jewelry for wood. They are a decorative woodworking technique that involves the insertion of one material into a recessed area of another to create intricate patterns, designs, or images (for example you could create intricate floral motifs, geometric patterns, intricate borders, or even personalized designs like initials or logos). This technique has been used for centuries to add elegance and visual interest to various woodworking projects such as furniture, flooring, musical instruments, and decorative panels. The choice of materials, colors, and shapes allows for customization and creative expression: they can be made from contrasting wood species, metals, or even mother-of-pearl. Experiment with geometric patterns, organic shapes, or intricate designs to add a touch of opulence to your joinery!

To create precise and clean inlays, woodworkers often use dedicated tools like inlay routers, chisels, coping saws or carving tools. Precision and patience are essential skills when working with inlays, as achieving a seamless fit and avoiding gaps or irregularities can be challenging.

Here below some of the main inlay techniques

1. **Marquetry.** This technique has a rich history dating back to ancient Egypt and has been used to adorn furniture, musical instruments, and even architectural features in palaces and cathedrals. It involves cutting thin sheets or veneers of different woods or materials into intricate shapes and then fitting them together to form a larger pattern. In traditional marquetry, artisans cut veneers into precise shapes and assemble them like

pieces of a jigsaw puzzle to form intricate patterns or scenes; the veneers are then glued onto a substrate, typically a solid wood base. Then we have the so-called Double-Bevel Cutting that is a technique that involves cutting each veneer piece at a slight angle (double bevel) to create a snug fit with adjacent pieces in order to ensure a seamless appearance in the finished work. Here I want to mention also the "Sand shading technique", a method used to add depth and shading to marquetry designs that involves lightly scorching the edges of veneer pieces with heated sand to create gradations in color.

Marquetry allows for an extensive range of design possibilities, from intricate floral motifs and pictorial scenes to geometric patterns and abstract compositions. Artisans often draw inspiration from nature, historical themes, or their own creativity, but of course this requires a high degree of craftsmanship and also some specific tools (for example a Fret Saw, a fine-toothed fret saw is used to cut veneer pieces precisely).

2. **Parquetry:** Similar to marquetry, Parquetry is a woodworking technique that involves the intricate arrangement of small wood pieces to create decorative geometric patterns or designs on the surface of floors, furniture, and other wooden objects.

3. **Intarsia:** Unlike marquetry, which focuses on creating patterns and designs using veneers, intarsia emphasizes creating detailed images and scenes by shaping and fitting solid pieces of wood together. It relies on the natural colors and grains of different wood species to create contrasting elements within the design (especially walnut, oak, maple, cherry and pine).

4. **Stringing and Banding:** In this technique, thin strips of contrasting materials are inlaid around the edges of furniture pieces or surfaces to create decorative borders.

Combining Multiple Joints

Sometimes, a single joint just won't cut it. Combining multiple joints not only enhances the structural integrity of your projects but also opens up a world of design possibilities. Here's some useful tips on how to do it:

1. Plan Your Joinery: Start by carefully planning which joints will work best for each part of your project. For instance, consider using dado joints for shelves, dovetail joints for corners, and mortise and tenon joints for frames.

2. Accurate Measuring: Precision is key when combining multiple joints, so make sure each joint fits perfectly by carefully measuring and marking your wood.

3. Gluing Sequence: Take care to glue the joints in the correct order while putting together your project. In a cabinet, for instance, it's common practice to put together the frame before attaching the shelves with dado joints.

4. Clamping and Drying: a strong bond can only be achieved with proper clamping: while the glue is drying, secure the joints with clamps. Take your time because a good connection requires time to dry.

Joinery for Curved and Irregular Shapes

Crafting joinery for curved and irregular shapes is like sculpting with wood. Whether crafting a flowing, organic chair design or curving inlays on a tabletop, each project has challenged me to think beyond straight lines and right angles, embracing the unique character of wood.

1. **Understand the Wood:** Wood has a natural tendency to bend and curve in certain directions due to its grain. Study the wood's grain pattern to determine how it will behave when shaped.

2. **Steam Bending:** Steam bending is a technique that involves heating the wood until it becomes pliable and then bending it into the desired shape. This method works well for creating curved components like chair legs or musical instrument parts.

3. **Laminated Wood:** For irregular shapes, laminating thin strips of wood together can be a powerful technique: by layering and gluing the strips, you can create complex and curved forms that are both strong and visually captivating.

4. **Carving and Sculpting:** Embrace the art of carving and sculpting to shape wood into irregular forms. Whether it's hand-carved joints or intricate, sculptural components, the process allows you to bring out the natural beauty of wood while achieving your desired shape.

Chapter 9: finishing techniques

Understanding wood finishing

Any seasoned woodworker will tell you that it takes more than just carpentry skills to transform raw lumber into a polished work of art. In fact there is another essential, often underestimated phase: the art of wood finishing.

Suppose you took a gorgeous piece of wood and meticulously turned it into a magnificent dining table. The grain moves like music, and the joints are flawless. But here's the catch: that table is still a delicate and susceptible work of art until it's given the proper finish. It's like having a diamond in the rough that is waiting to shine. Preservation, protection, and efficiency are equally important considerations here.

Because it is a natural substance with a life cycle, wood may be damaged by weather. Without a finish to preserve it, it can easily distort, crack, or deteriorate over time. The wood's beauty and durability are protected by a coat of finish that will last for many years....we can say that finishing is like arming your woodworking projects with a shield able to protect your projects against the elements, sunlight, stains, and general wear and tear. It's what separates an item that ages well from one that deteriorates quickly.

The correct coating not only protects, but also improves. The grain of the wood may be highlighted, the color intensified, and the wood's natural beauty emphasized. It's the finishing touch that takes your handiwork from great to truly jaw-dropping.

Tips for Selecting the Right Finish for Specific Wood Species

Just as a sommelier pairs wine with cuisine, a woodworker pairs finishes with specific wood species. The right finish can enhance the wood's innate qualities, transforming it into a masterpiece. Here are some tips to help you make the perfect pairing:

1. Understand Wood Species: Each wood species possesses unique characteristics, from grain patterns to color variations. Take the time to understand the wood you're working with, as this will influence your finish selection.

2. Consider the Desired Look: Are you aiming for a rustic, natural appearance, or do you want to deepen the wood's color and add a glossy sheen? Your desired look will dictate the finish.

3. Test Samples: Always test a small sample of the wood with your chosen finish before committing to the entire project. This allows you to see how the finish will interact with the wood and ensures you achieve the desired result.

4. Match the Finish to the Project's Use: Consider the environment and purpose of your woodworking creation. Will it be indoors or outdoors? Subject to heavy use or occasional display? The finish should be tailored to the project's intended use.

5. Balance Aesthetics and Protection: Striking the right balance between aesthetics and protection is key. Some finishes, like varnishes, offer excellent protection but may alter the wood's appearance. Others, like oils, enhance aesthetics but offer less protection.

6. Follow Application Instructions: Different finishes have specific application methods and drying times. Carefully follow the manufacturer's instructions to achieve the best results.

Types of Wood Finishes

Now, Let's dive into the diverse array of wood finishes, each with its own set of benefits, methods of application, and aesthetic outcomes. The choice of finish by a carpenter is analogous to the selection of paints and brushes by an artist.

1. Stains and Dyes: they function similarly to an artist's palette, improving the aesthetic value of wood by imparting additional hues and shadings. Dyes produce provide vibrant and uniform hues, while stains permeate the wood and highlight the grain. When selecting a stain or dye, it is important to take into account both the species of wood and the final desired hue.

2. Clear Finishes: Clear finishes such as varnishes, lacquers, and polyurethanes are like a protective glass case for your wood; they provide a transparent, glossy or matte layer that shields and accentuates the wood's character.

3. Oil Finishes: oil finishes such as linseed oil, tung oil, or Danish oil are your friends if you want to highlight the wood's innate beauty and warmth. They soak in deeply, bringing out the wood's natural beauty and intensifying its texture.

Linseed oil is derived from flaxseeds and provides a warm, amber-like finish; it also penetrates the wood's surface, protecting it from moisture and providing a natural sheen.

Tung oil is extracted from the nuts of the tung tree and provides a clear, natural finish that doesn't darken the wood as much as linseed oil; it has excellent water resistance and durability, making it suitable for both indoor and outdoor applications.

Danish oil is not a pure oil but a blend of various ingredients, typically including a combination of tung oil, linseed oil, and varnish or polyurethane. It combines the benefits of both tung and linseed oil with added protection from the varnish or polyurethane components, and provides a durable, water-resistant finish with a slight sheen. It is often considered easier to apply because it includes varnish or polyurethane, reducing the number of coats required for a protective finish.

4. Shellac and French Polishing: To those who appreciate the finer things in life, shellac and French polishing represent the pinnacle of sophistication. Shellac, which is made from resin, gives things an antique look and a warm amber color, while French polishing takes it to the next level, producing a high-gloss sheen.

5. Lacquer and Spray Finishing: Many woodworkers choose lacquers because to their quick drying time and remarkable durability. Spray finishing, which requires specialist equipment, produces a faultless, expert appearance, making it the go-to method for intricate projects.

6. Brushing Techniques: Sometimes, the human touch is essential. Brushing on finishes allows for precision and control, particularly in tight spaces or on smaller pieces. It's the equivalent of a skilled artist applying fine details to a canvas. This technique involves using a wire brush or a stiff bristle brush to remove softwood fibers from the surface of the wood. Brushing is often done after the wood has been sanded to open up the grain, expose the wood's natural texture, and create an attractive, weathered, or rustic look.

Surface preparation

Sanding: The Foundation of Wood Finishing

Often, when dealing with wood, after cutting and scraping the surface, the burs and splinters are not finished. This is a simple fix with fast sanding, but it can become complicated with an endless number of sandpaper and sanding equipment styles and grains. Belt sanders, orbit sanders, and manual sanders are the main types of sanders we are considering.

Sanding is fundamental to smooth out imperfections, but also to prepare the surface for optimal adhesion of the finish.

Whatever sander you have, sandpaper will be used. Most sandpapers are aluminum oxides and are available in various grains. The grain is an indicator of how fine it is and how well you use it. Grits typically range from 20 to 1000; 20 are highly racing, and 1000 are very fine.

- Sandpaper's big hitters are the coarse grits, which range from 40 to 60 on the grit scale. They are ideal for eliminating obstinate defects, leveling surfaces, and shaping wood, and come in a variety of shapes.
- Medium Grits (80-120): As we continue to work our way up the grit scale, we're starting to find our rhythm. When using medium grits, the surface of the wood is refined, and the rough edges that were left behind by using coarser grits are smoothed off.
- Fine Grits (150-220): At this point, we've reached the ideal consistency. The wood is prepared for finishing using fine grits, which results in a surface that is both touchable and ready to receive the transformative effects of wood finishes.
- Very Fine Grits (320-600): These are the virtuosos of sandpaper, polishing the wood to a velvety, satin-like surface. The grits range from very fine to extremely fine. They are an excellent choice for making final preparations before adding finishes such as stains, varnishes, or others.
- Extra-Fine Grits (800 and higher): Extra-fine grits are considered the crème de la crème of the sandpaper industry because they bring the wood to a degree of refinement that is so high that it is almost otherworldly. They provide a finish that is similar to a mirror, which is ideal for highlighting the wood's inherent attractiveness.

Now let's see some tips about the process.

First of all, to prevent gouging the wood or creating uneven surfaces, it is important to use pressure that is both even and soft. Imagine that it is more of a gentle caress than a firm hold on you rather than the alternative.

Keep a steady beat and go in the direction of the wood grain while you're doing this step. Following the grain's natural flow is similar to the way a pianist would play in harmony with the song if they did so.

Consider a gradual progression: after addressing defects with coarser grits, go through the grits in a progressive way, polishing the surface with each pass as you go. It's quite similar to how a crescendo is built up in a symphony.

You should be careful not to oversand the surface. Sanding too much with a fine grit can cause the pores in the wood to shut, which makes it less responsive to stains and finishes.

Filling Wood Pores and Imperfections

Wood pores, those minuscule openings in the wood's surface, can be a source of character or a nuisance, depending on your perspective. They absorb finishes differently, which can result in uneven coloring. To fill wood pores:

1. **Grain Filler:** These are thick, paste-like substances that are worked into the wood's pores. Once dry, excess filler is sanded away, leaving a smooth surface ready for finishing.

2. **Putty or Wood Filler:** Putties or fillers, available in different colors to match the wood you are working with, are used to fill small imperfections like cracks, nail holes or knots. They're applied, dried, and sanded flush with the wood's surface.

3. **Clear Grain Filler:** If you want to maintain the wood's natural color, opt for a clear grain filler that doesn't alter the wood's hue.

Stains and Dyes

Early in my woodworking journey, I embarked on a project using a stunning piece of cherry wood. The grain was mesmerizing, and I had big plans for this piece—a deep, lustrous finish that would accentuate the wood's natural beauty.

With a certain enthusiasm, I applied the stain directly to the cherry wood, expecting to witness an immediate transformation...but what I saw left me bewildered and frustrated: the color appeared uneven, with some areas absorbing the stain intensely, while others seemed reluctant to change. My dream of a flawless finish was in jeopardy!

Pre-stain conditioning, which I learned about in my search for a way to save my project, involves treating wood with a particular solution before applying stain. This product, known as a pre-stain wood conditioner, is used to permeate the wood's surface and normalize the wood's absorption rate before applying stain. Because wood is a porous natural material, it doesn't take stain consistently. It's possible that certain places are more permeable or absorbent than others, resulting in blotchy or uneven coloring. Sealing pores and encouraging uniformity are two of the many benefits pre-stain conditioners provide.

You should apply it after sanding, using a brush, rag, or sponge, apply the pre-stain conditioner generously to the wood's surface. Ensure even coverage. Let the conditioner sit for the specified time indicated on the product's label in order to penetrate and do its magic, then remove any residue with a clean towel. The wood should feel slightly damp but not wet. Now that the wood has been cleaned and conditioned, you may start staining it. You'll see that the stain is absorbed more regularly and uniformly, producing the required color consistency.

Choosing Between Stains and Dyes

Should you opt for wood stains or wood dyes? Much like a painter deciding between oil and watercolor, this choice depends on the effect you aim to achieve and the type of wood you're working with.

Stains: Wood stains are pigmented solutions that contain both color and a binder. They provide a more substantial, semi-opaque finish. Stains are great for modifying the color of wood without completely altering its appearance, highlighting the wood's grain and emphasizing its depth. Oak and mahogany, which have especially visible grain patterns, are ideal for this.

Dyes: Wood dyes, on the other hand, are typically translucent solutions that go deep into the wood's fibers. They offer vibrant, transparent coloration, and are great for coloring woods uniformly and vividly, especially those with a fine grain like maple and cherry.

When applying wood stain, remember that patience and precision are your allies. Here are two common application techniques:

- **Brush or Rag Application:** Use a brush or a clean cloth to apply the stain evenly along the wood's grain. Allow the stain to penetrate for a few minutes before wiping off any excess with a clean cloth. This method offers control and precision.
- **Spray Application:** if you are working on larger/intricate surfaces, I suggest using a spray gun to apply the stain in order to ensure even coverage and be more efficient.

Depending on the depth of color you desire, you can apply multiple coats of stain. Each additional coat deepens the color, so experiment to achieve the perfect hue.

Custom Shades

The ability to mix wood stains to produce a unique shade is fascinating, much like how a painter mixes colors on a palette to get a new hue: this opens up a realm of artistic possibilities, allowing you to match existing woodwork, achieve unique effects, or simply let your imagination run wild.

1. Start with a Base Stain: Pick a basic stain that will be the basis for your final color (it should be a near approximation of the final hue).

2. Experiment: Begin blending by adding small amounts of another stain color to your base stain. Mix thoroughly and test the result on a scrap piece of wood. Remember to keep track of your proportions and the order in which you add stains to replicate the custom shade later.

3. Test and Adjust: Continue experimenting until you achieve the desired color. Remember that you can always make the color darker but making it lighter is much trickier. Once you've found the perfect shade, take note of your stain blend proportions.

4. Apply the Custom Shade: With your custom stain blend in hand, apply it to your. You'll now have a finish that is uniquely yours.

Clear Finishes

Imagine clear finishes as the guardians of wood's beauty, shielding it from the elements while enhancing its visual allure. Each member of this trio—varnishes, lacquers, and polyurethanes—brings its own strengths and character to the stage.

1. Varnishes: Varnishes, the classic stalwarts of clear finishes, are known for their exceptional durability and protective qualities, in fact they deposit a protective layer that is resistant to moisture, chemicals, and wear. Moreover they accentuate the wood's natural color, giving it a warm, golden tone that intensifies over time; their heavier texture, however, makes them more difficult to apply evenly.

2. Lacquers: Lacquers are well known for their user-friendliness and the speed with which they dry. They provide a very smooth, transparent, and long-lasting coating, and, unlike varnishes, that leave an amber tint to the wood, lacquers are often water-clear. Although lacquers are suitable for interior usage or more protected outdoor applications, they may not be as water-resistant as varnishes or polyurethanes.

3. Polyurethanes: Polyurethanes have an excellent combination of toughness and adaptability, in fact they can be used for a wide range of projects thanks to the fact that they come in both water-based and oil-based formulas. Polyurethane coatings, whether clear or amber in color, provide outstanding resistance against moisture, abrasion, and UV rays. Many people who work with wood prefer water-based types because they dry quickly and produce less odors when applied.

Application Methods and Tips: Crafting a Flawless Finish

Applying clear finishes is not merely a task; it's an art form that demands attention to detail and finesse. Here are some methods and tips to achieve a flawless finish that accentuates the wood's beauty:

1. Surface Preparation: The surface must be properly prepared before applying any coating. Remove any rough spots or blemishes from the wood by sanding it and ensure to get rid of any dirt or dust that may be on the wood.

2. Thin Coats: When applying clear finishes, it's better to use multiple thin coats rather than a single heavy coat because coats that are applied thinly dry more quickly, prevent the finish from running or dripping, and allow for more precise application.

3. Brushing: Brushing is a common method for applying clear finishes. If you are applying an oil-based finish, use a brush with natural bristles, however if you are using a water-based finish, use a brush with synthetic bristles. Apply the finish in the direction of the wood grain, using long, even strokes, following the directions provided by the manufacturer.

4. Spraying: Spraying may be an effective procedure, particularly when applied to larger projects or ones that require a very flawless finish. It gives an equal coating and reduces the appearance of brush strokes even if, on the other hand, it can call for specialist equipment as well as enough ventilation.

5. Sanding Between Coats: Sand lightly between coats using fine-grit sandpaper (usually 220-grit or higher) in order to remove any imperfections and provides better adhesion for subsequent coats.

Achieving the Perfect Sheen: Satin, Semi-Gloss, and High Gloss
The sheen of a clear finish plays a significant role in the overall aesthetics of a woodworking project. It can range from a soft, subtle glow to a mirror-like brilliance. Here are the most common sheen options:

1. Satin: Satin finishes offer a soft, low-luster sheen and provide a warm and elegant look that is less reflective than higher-gloss solutions; these ones are excellent for projects where you want to highlight the wood's natural beauty while minimizing glare and imperfections.

2. Semi-Gloss: Semi-gloss finishes are the perfect a balance between shine and subtlety, because they offer a moderate level of reflection, providing a smooth and polished appearance. They are versatile and work well for a wide range of projects.

3. High Gloss: Shine and reflection are at their pinnacle in surfaces that have been finished with a high gloss. Woodworking projects benefit from increased drama and aesthetic impact when they have a surface that is glossy and reflective like a mirror: when a daring and eye-catching appearance is needed for a piece, a high gloss finish is usually selected as the best option.

The choice of sheen is heavily influenced by both your own personal taste and the specifics of the project you're working on. Finishes with a satin or semi-gloss sheen are frequently used for furniture and other interior applications, but finishes with a high gloss sheen have the potential to steal the show on particular pieces, such as ornamental objects and specialty items.

Specialty Finishing Techniques

There are some specialty finishing techniques that, to me, are nothing short of magic, allowing artisans to transcend the ordinary and infuse their creations with character, depth and a piece of their creative soul.

Distressing and antiquing wood

Distressing wood involves simulating the wear and tear that occurs naturally over time. Here your goal is to create subtle imperfections, such as dents, scratches, and small cracks, that mimic the signs of genuine aging. The process of antiquing wood goes one step farther than distressing it by using processes that imitate the patina and character seen on antique furniture, and this results in the wood having an aged and somewhat faded look, giving the impression that it has elegantly withstood years of usage. These techniques are like a portal to the past, allowing me to craft pieces that resonate with history. As I work, I can't help but wonder about the stories this wood could tell, the places it has been, and the hands that have touched it.

Among the method to distress wood we have:

- **Sandpaper and Tools:** Use sandpaper, chisels, chains, hammers, or even rocks can be used to create a distressed look on the surface of the wood. Pay attention to the edges, corners, and other places that would normally experience wear.
- **Stain and Paint:** After applying a coat of stain or paint, sand away portions of it in predetermined locations to expose the underlying wood. This method, often known as "chippy paint," creates the impression that there are several layers of old paint on the surface.
- **Dye and Water:** Wood may be given the impression of having been used for a long time by applying water spots and stains made from a mixture of wood dye and water.

Here's how to antique wood:

- **Glazing:** Apply a glaze, that usually is a mixture of paint and a transparent medium, over the wood. The glaze settles into crevices and corners, highlighting details and creating depth.
- **Aging Agents:** Personally I often use aging agents like vinegar and steel wool to artificially age wood, giving it a slightly weathered look; thanks to this solution the wood emerges with an elegance that speaks of enduring beauty, an artful testament to its history.
- **Wax and Rubbing:** Apply a dark furniture wax and rub it into the wood, then buff it off in order to create a subtle aged sheen.

Creating Custom Finishes

Imagine having the power to craft custom finishes that are uniquely yours! Glazes, already mentioned for the antiquing process, are translucent mixtures of paint and a glazing medium that are applied over a base finish and allow me to add depth and drama to my work.

Toners are another fascinating way to customize wood finishes. They are mixtures of paint or dye and a clear base that add a subtle hue to the wood, enhancing its color and creating a harmonious, uniform appearance. To get the desired result, you may need to apply many coats of toner in order to achieve the desired depth of color. Wait for each layer to dry completely before proceeding to the next; then, after you have reached the correct shade, you should safeguard the toner by sealing the finish with a clear topcoat. This will bring out its full potential.

Accentuating grain patterns is yet another finishing method that you might experiment with in order to give your product a more unique appearance; to me, this is a form of devotion when it comes to my passion for woodworking! Wood is a canvas with its own story to tell, marked by figure and grain patterns that are unique to each species and accentuating these natural characteristics is an art form in itself, allowing any woodworker to celebrate the inherent beauty of the material:

- **Figure Enhancement:** Figure in wood refers to distinctive patterns or visual effects caused by irregularities in the grain. Techniques like using contrasting stains or dyes, applying toners, or using specialized figure-enhancing finishes can bring out the figure's beauty and depth.

- **Grain Emphasis:** The grain of the wood is its fingerprint, and it can be accentuated by applying several techniques, for example raising the grain and sanding with the grain are both options that allow you to enhance the wood's texture; alternatively you can apply clear finishes like Danish oil or tung oil to deepen the grain's appearance while preserving its natural color

Finishing Outdoor Wood

The art of finishing outdoor wood is not just about aesthetics; it's a practical endeavor to ensure longevity and resilience. In fact, in the open embrace of the elements, wood can become vulnerable, weathered, and dull over time...When used outdoors, it is engaged in a constant battle with Mother Nature: sunlight, rain, snow, humidity, and temperature fluctuations...all elements take their toll. To protect outdoor wood, you must understand the nature of the enemy:

1. UV Rays: The sun's ultraviolet (UV) rays are relentless foes, causing wood to fade, discolor and even crack over time. UV protection is essential for preserving the wood's color and structural integrity.

2. Moisture and Mold: Rain and humidity can lead to moisture absorption, which, in turn, fosters the growth of mold, mildew, and rot. Keeping wood dry and well-ventilated is crucial.

3. Temperature Swings: Rapid changes in temperature can cause wood to expand and contract, potentially leading to warping and splitting.

4. Insects and Pests: Wood-boring insects and pests can wreak havoc on outdoor wood structures. Proper protection is essential to deter these invaders.

Selecting the appropriate finish for your outdoor woodwork is akin to choosing armor for a knight, it's a decision that will determine the wood's fate in the face of the elements. Here are some options to consider:

1. Exterior Stains: Exterior wood stains are formulated to penetrate the wood's surface, providing protection while allowing the natural beauty of the wood to shine through. They come in various levels of transparency, from clear to solid color, allowing you to choose how much of the wood's grain you want to reveal.

2. Paint: Paint offers strong protection against UV rays and moisture, making it a formidable choice for outdoor projects. However, it conceals the wood's natural grain and texture, creating a more uniform appearance.

3. Water-Based Finishes: Water-based finishes, available in clear and tinted options, are environmentally friendly and have low VOC (volatile organic compound) emissions. They are a good choice for those seeking a more eco-conscious solution.

4. Oil-Based Finishes: Oil-based finishes provide excellent durability and protection and have the ability to enhance the wood's natural color and beauty; they are particularly effective at repelling water and preventing cracking and splitting.

5. Varnish: Varnish is frequently used on wooden surfaces that are exposed to the elements and require a finish that is both glossy and long-lasting. It offers protection in the form of a glossy covering that is resistant to harm from both water and ultraviolet light.

Chapter 10: Super easy projects to reinforce your skills

Project 1: Wooden Shelf

Materials Needed:
- 1x6 or 1x8 pine boards (length is up to you, as it depends on the shelf you want to build)
- Wood glue
- Screws
- Sandpaper
- Wood finish (stain or paint)
- Mounting brackets (optional)

Instructions:
1. **Measure and Cut** - Measure the desired length for your shelf, then use a miter saw or handsaw to cut the pine board to the measured length: you have just built the shelf's top surface.
2. **Prepare the Backing** - Cut another piece of pine board to the same length as the shelf. This will be the backing for your shelf.
3. **Attach the Backing** - Spread wood glue along the perimeter of the backing piece, then push it firmly on the underside of the shelf. Ensure the pieces are flush at one end, creating an L-shaped bracket.
4. **Secure with Screws** – Now you should secure the backing to the shelf by using screws. First, drill pilot holes into the wood to prevent the wood from breaking, and then drive screws through the backing and into the shelf.
5. **Sand and Finish** - Sand the whole shelf, making sure to round off any edges that are pointed. Apply a coat of paint or stain, whatever you like, and then wait until it has completely dried before proceeding.
6. **Mount the Shelf** - Mounting brackets should be used in order to keep the shelf in place on the wall. Remember to make sure to attach them to wall studs for stability.

Project 2: Wooden Plant Stand

Materials Needed:

- 2x2 pine boards (length depends on desired stand height)
- Wood glue
- Screws
- Sandpaper
- Wood finish (stain or paint)

Instructions:

1. **Cut the Legs** - Measure and cut 4 pieces of identical length from the 2x2 pine boards in order to build the legs of your plant stand. The exact length depends on how tall you want the stand to be.

2. **Cut the Top** - To serve as the top surface of your plant stand, cut a square or circular piece of plywood or pine board. The dimensions of the stand need to be determined with reference to the size of the pot that will be placed on it.

3. **Assemble the Frame:** Arrange the 4 legs to form a square or round frame, then apply wood glue to the ends and connect them at right angles in order to create corners. Screws should be used to secure the joints.

4. **Attach the Top** - After applying wood glue to the top edges of the legs, position the wooden top so that it sits atop the legs. Ensure that it is centered, and then fasten it with screws inserted from the bottom.

5. **Sand and Finish** - Sand the whole plant stand so that any sharp edges are smoothed off. You may complete it by staining it or painting it, whatever you like. Please allow it to dry completely.

Project 3: Wooden Coasters

Materials Needed:

- 4x4 pine posts or small wooden squares
- Wood glue
- Sandpaper
- Wood finish (stain or paint)

Instructions:

1. **Cut the Coasters** - Measure and cut the 4x4 pine posts into smaller, square pieces (usually around 4x4 inches apiece) by using either a miter saw or handsaw.
2. **Sand the Edges** - Sand all the edges of the wooden squares so that any sharp corners or edges are rounded off.
3. **Design or Patterns (Optional)** - If desired, You may either use a woodburning tool or paint to create beautiful designs or patterns on the coasters.
4. **Finish** – Now you can apply a wood finish, such as stain or paint, to protect the coasters and enhance their appearance. Allow them to dry completely.
5. **Add Felt Pads** - In order to prevent the coasters from scratching surfaces, attach felt pads to the underside of each one.

Project 4: Wooden Photo Frame

Materials Needed:

- 1x4 pine boards (length depends on frame size)
- Wood glue
- Miter saw or handsaw
- Sandpaper
- Wood finish (stain or paint)
- Glass or acrylic sheet (cut to frame size)
- Backing board (cut to frame size)
- Picture hangers or wire

Instructions:

1. **Measure and Cut** - Take accurate measurements of the piece of artwork or photograph that will be framed, then cut 4 pieces of 1x4 pine to build the frame, making 45-degree miter cuts at each end to form the corners.
2. **Assemble the Frame** - Now consider the mitered ends and join them using wood glue to obtain the frame. Until it is completely dry, use clamps to hold the corners in place.
3. **Sand and Finish** - Sand the frame so that any jagged edges are removed; after applying the wood finish of your choosing, allow it to dry completely.
4. **Add Glass and Backing** - Once the frame is dry, insert the glass or acrylic sheet and the backing board. Secure them in place.
5. **Attach Picture Hangers** - Attach picture hangers or wire to the back of the frame for hanging.

Project 5: Wooden Serving Tray

Materials Needed:

- 1x6 or 1x8 pine boards (length depends on tray size)
- Wood glue
- Screws
- Sandpaper
- Wood finish (stain or paint)
- Cabinet handles (optional)

Instructions:

1. **Measure and Cut** - Create the base and sides of your serving tray out of pine boards by first measuring and then cutting them to size. The dimensions of the tray you want will determine the size you need.
2. **Assemble the Tray** - After applying wood glue around the borders of the bottom piece, you can next join the side pieces to create a tray that is either rectangular or square in shape. Screws should be used to secure the joints.
3. **Reinforce the Corners** - Mitering the corners of the tray by cutting them at a 45-degree angle gives the tray more structural support and provides a decorative feature.
4. **Sand and Finish** - Sand the entire tray to ensure smooth edges and surfaces. Apply the type of wood finish that you find most appealing.
5. **Add Handles (Optional)** - If desired, you could consider to attach cabinet handles to the sides of the tray for easy carrying.

Project 6: Wooden Key Holder

Materials Needed:

- 1x4 pine board (length depends on the number of hooks)
- Wood glue
- Screws
- Sandpaper
- Wood finish (stain or paint)
- Key hooks

Instructions:

1. **Measure and Cut** - Decide how long you would like your key holder to be, then cut a piece of pine board measuring 1 by 4 inches to that length.
2. **Design the Key Hooks** - First, choose how many key hooks you want on your holder, and then mark places around the board so that they are evenly spaced; now pre-drill small holes at these points.
3. **Attach the Hooks** - Simply screw the key hooks into the holes that have been pre-drilled, and check to see that they are hooked on tightly.
4. **Sand and Finish** - Sand the entire key holder to remove any rough edges and apply the type of wood finish that you find most appealing.
5. **Mount the Holder** - Attach the key holder to the wall using screws or mounting hardware, making sure it's at a convenient height for hanging keys.

Chapter 11: Step-by-step projects for the weekend woodworker

VEGETABLE STORAGE CASE

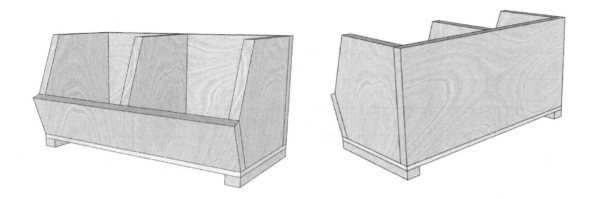

EXPLODED VIEW – EACH PIECE IDENTIFIED

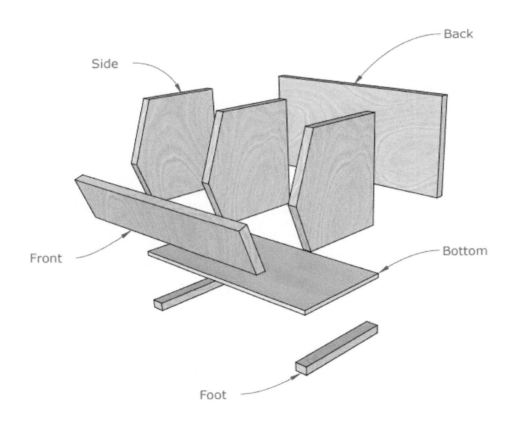

Back

Side

Front

Bottom

Foot

Material list

Part	Description	Quantity	Length	Width	Thickness	Material
A	Front	1	12 1/2"	2 11/16"	1/2"	1/2" Plywood
B	Side	3	6"	5 11/16"	1/2"	1/2" Plywood
C	Back	1	12 1/2"	6"	1/2"	1/2" Plywood
D	Bottom	1	12 1/2"	5 13/16"	1/4"	1/4" Plywood
E	Foot	2	5 13/16"	3/4"	1/2"	1/2" Plywood

Step 1 – Cut each piece.

All parts are cut from 1/2"-thick plywood. See drawing below.

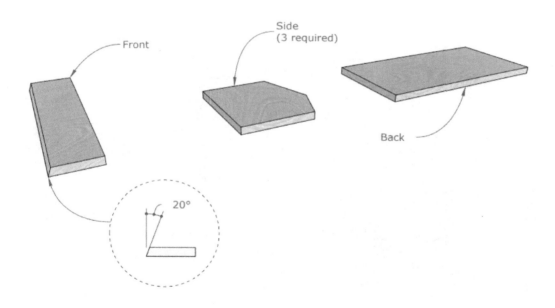

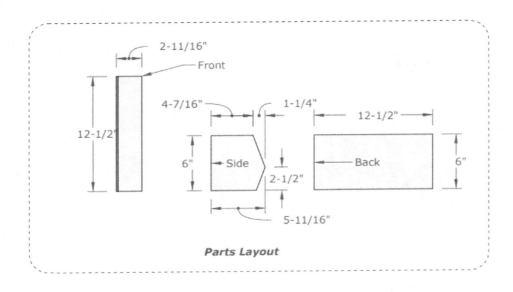

Parts Layout

STEP 2 – Assemble the case.

Put all the pieces in place, apply glue clamp, and let it dry. Make sure everything is squared.

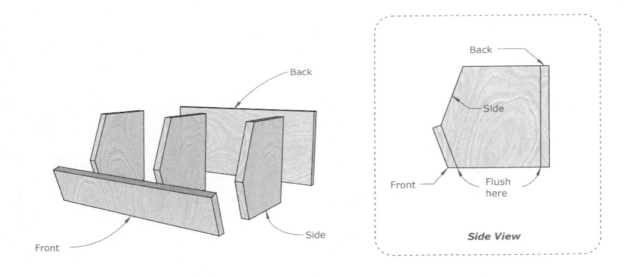

Side View

119

STEP 3 – Bottom is attached.

Insert the bottom by gluing or nailing it in place.

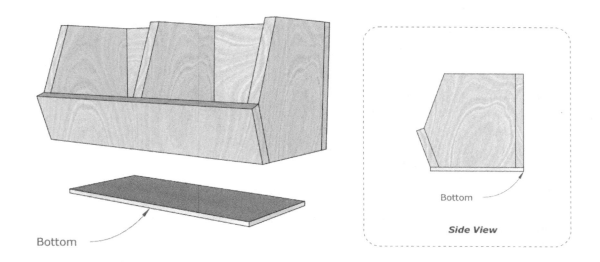

STEP 4 – Attach the feet.

Finally, attach the two feet. Glue or nail them to the bottom.

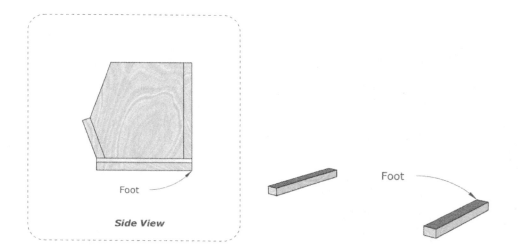

BOOK ORGANIZER

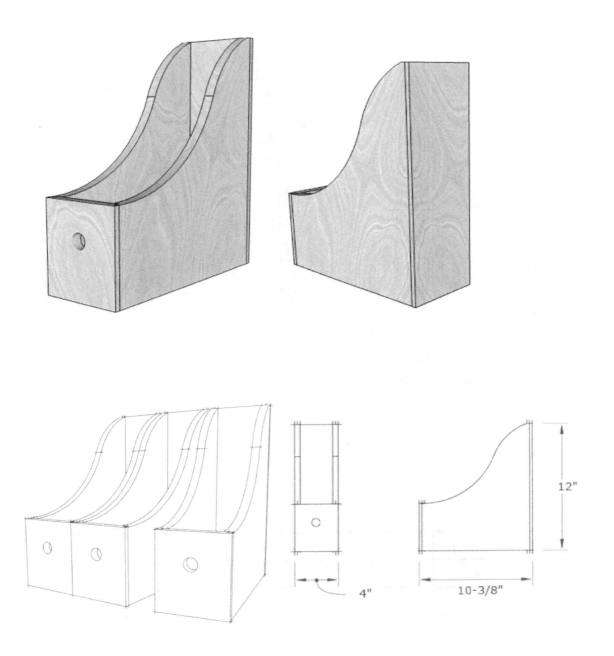

4"

12"

10-3/8"

EXPLODED VIEW – EACH PIECE IDENTIFIED

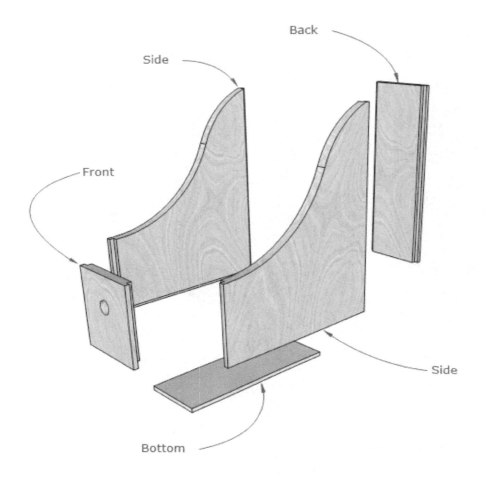

Material list

Part	Description	Quantity	Length	Width	Thickness	Material
A	Front	1	4 1/2"	4"	1/2"	1/2 Plywood
B	Side	2	12"	9 7/8"	1/2"	1/2 Plywood
C	Back	1	12"	4"	1/2"	1/2 Plywood
D	Bottom	1	9 5/8"	3 1/2"	1/4"	1/4 Plywood

STEP 1 - Cut each piece.

All parts are cut from 1/2"-thick veneer plywood. See drawing below. Cut the 1/4" rabbets as shown.

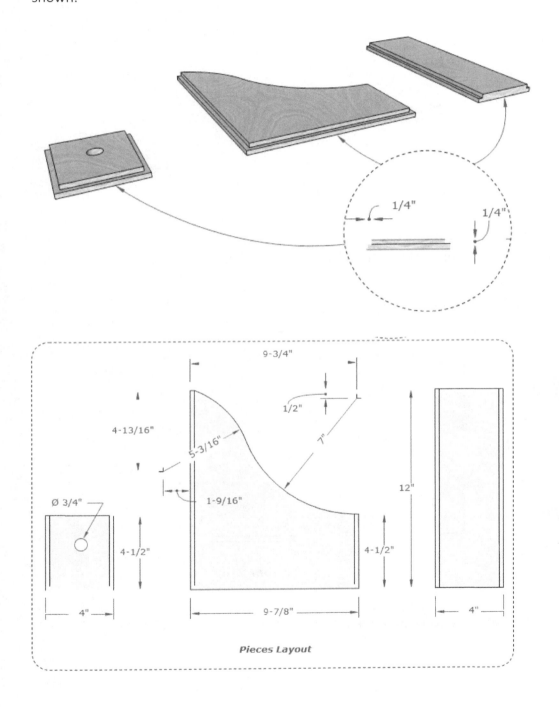

Pieces Layout

STEP 2 – Assemble the case. Put all the pieces in place, apply glue clamp, and let it dry. Make sure everything is squared.

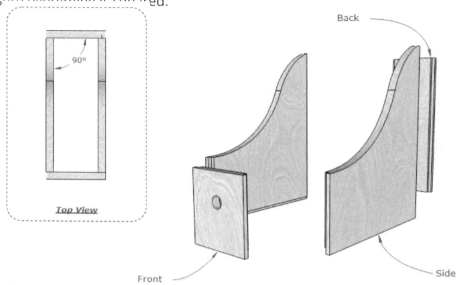

STEP 3 – Put bottom in place. Insert the bottom by gluing or nailing it in place.

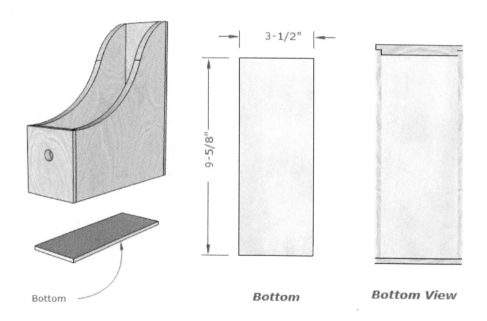

STEP 4 – Apply your finish. Now you can tackle the clutter with your new book organizer!

CAMP CHAIR

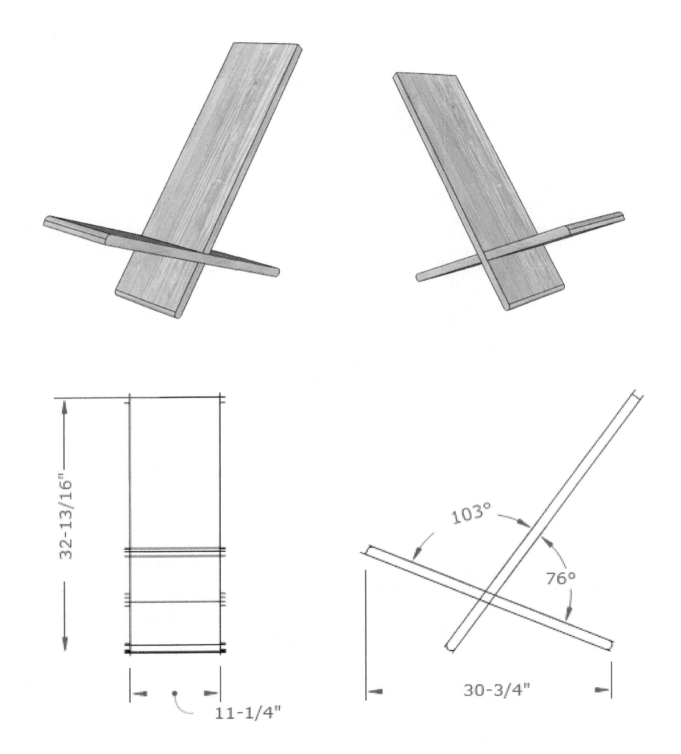

32-13/16"

11-1/4"

103°

76°

30-3/4"

EXPLODED VIEW – EACH PIECE IDENTIFIED

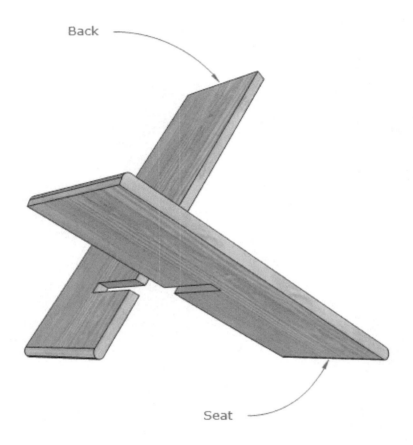

Back

Seat

Material List

Part	Description	Quantity	Length	Width	Thickness	Material
A	Seat	1	33"	11 1/4"	1/4"	2x12 Wood
B	Back	1	40"	11 1/4"	1/4"	2x12 Wood

STEP 1 – Cut the seat.

The camp chair is made of two boards with an edge lap joint.

Cut the seat board to size, cut the notch, and round the ends as shown below.

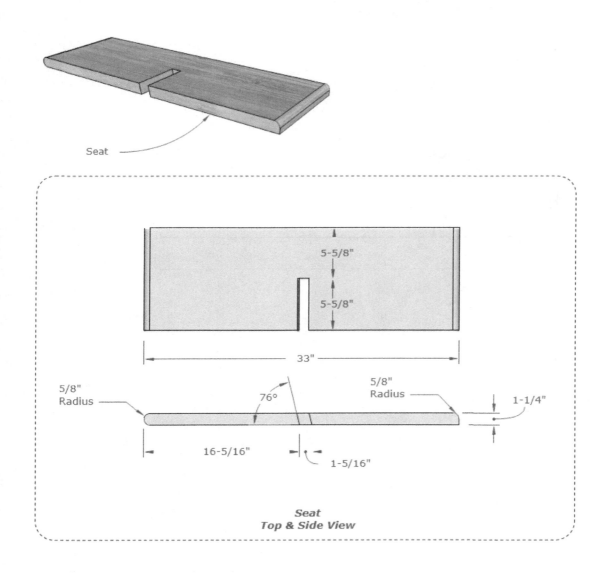

Seat
Top & Side View

STEP 2 – Cut the back.

Cut the back board to size, cut the notch, and round the ends as shown below.

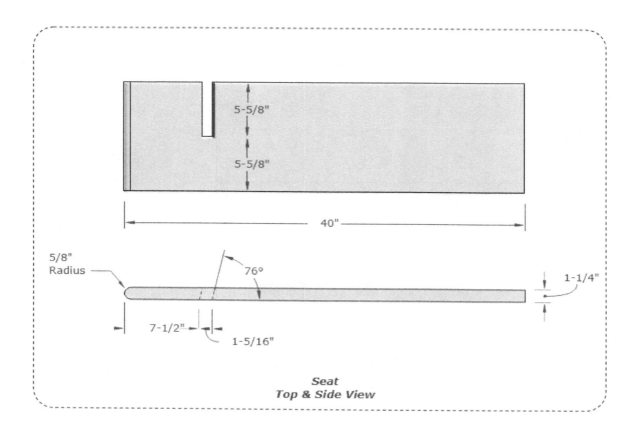

5-5/8"

5-5/8"

40"

5/8"
Radius

76°

1-1/4"

7-1/2"

1-5/16"

Seat
Top & Side View

STEP 3 – Assemble the seat.

Slide the pieces together.

STEP 4 – Apply your finish.

Finally, when the two pieces are put together you can apply the desired finish.

COFFEE TABLE

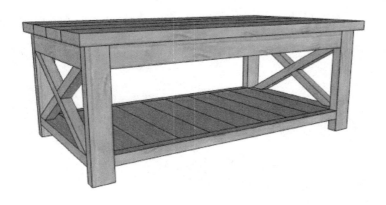

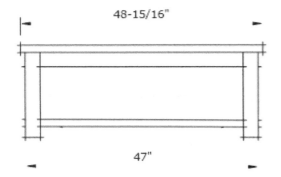

48-15/16"

47"

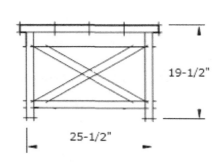

19-1/2"

25-1/2"

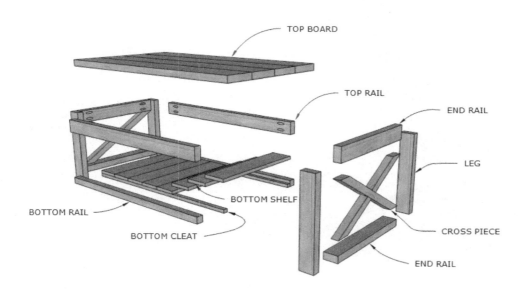

TOP BOARD

TOP RAIL

END RAIL

LEG

CROSS PIECE

BOTTOM SHELF

BOTTOM RAIL

BOTTOM CLEAT

END RAIL

Material List

Parts	Description	Quantity	Length	Width	Thickness
A	LEG	4	18"	3"	1 1/2"
B	TOP RAIL	2	41"	3"	1 1/2"
C	BOTTOM RAIL	2	41"	1 1/2"	1 1/2"
D	END RAIL	4	22 1/2"	3"	1 1/2"
E	BOTTOM CLEAT	2	41"	1"	3/4"
F	CROSS PIECE	4	25 1/8"	1 1/2"	1 1/2"
G	TOP BOARD	6	42"	5"	1 1/2"
H	BOTTOM SHELF	8	22 1/2"	5 1/8"	3/4"

Front and back - Drill pocket holes and assemble front and back frames using 2 1/2" Pocket Hole screws.

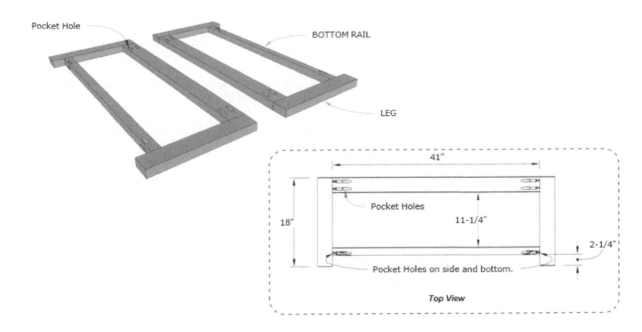

End rails - Turn them over and attach side boards to the back frame using 2 1/2" Pocket Hole screws.

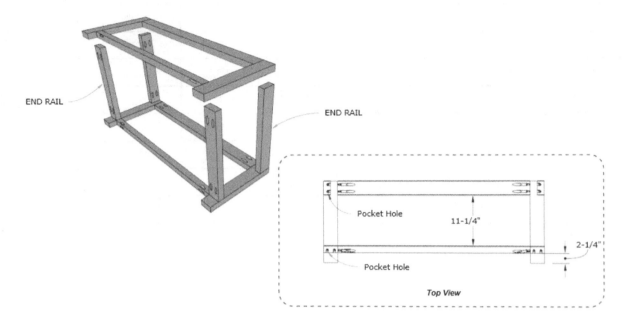

Bottom cleat:

The bottom cleat sits 3/4" below the top of the bottom rail, allowing the shelf to sit flush.

The screws are inserted on the 3/4" side. Predrilled and spaced 8" apart. Use 1 1/2" screws.

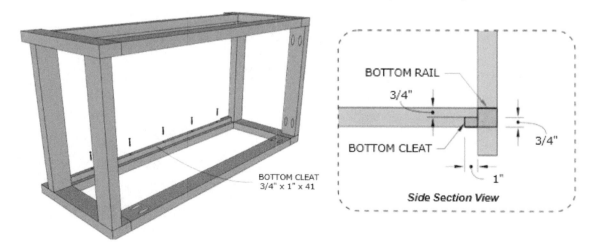

Cross pieces:

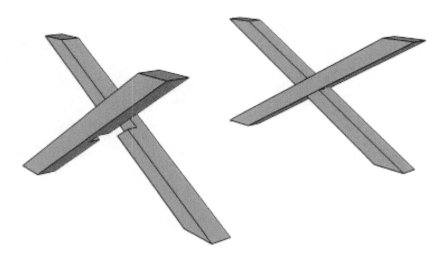

Trim them all to roughly 26" in length.

The process of joining these cross pieces starts by cutting angled half laps in all of the strips. See set up below (a). Fit the strips together with glue and clamps.

With the cross pieces assembled, trim them to the correct width and length in order to fit inside the legs. See detail (b).

Draw a template on a piece of plywood as a guide for cutting and checking the fit of the parts. See diagram (b).

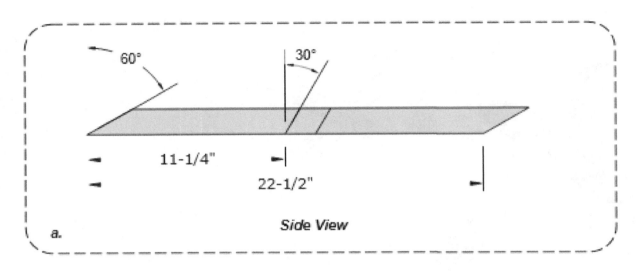

60°

30°

11-1/4"

22-1/2"

Side View

a.

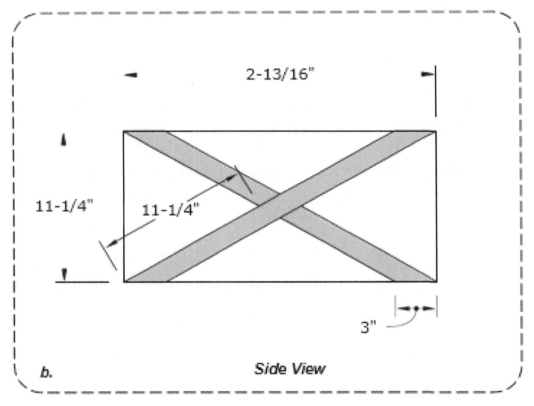

2-13/16"

11-1/4"

11-1/4"

3"

Side View

b.

Attach cross pieces:

Install X frame either by using half tap method or cut and screw from the back.

Tip: If using locks, leave one end open until the bottom board is installed as the final step.

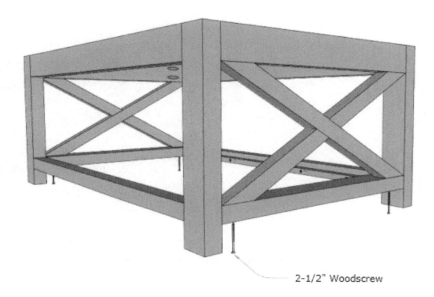

2-1/2" Woodscrew

Build the tabletop:

Build the top board to the correct dimensions. Drill pocket holes on the boards with 6" spacing (see figure), glue and screw using 1 1/2" Pocket Hole screws.

Distress, paint, or stain at this point.

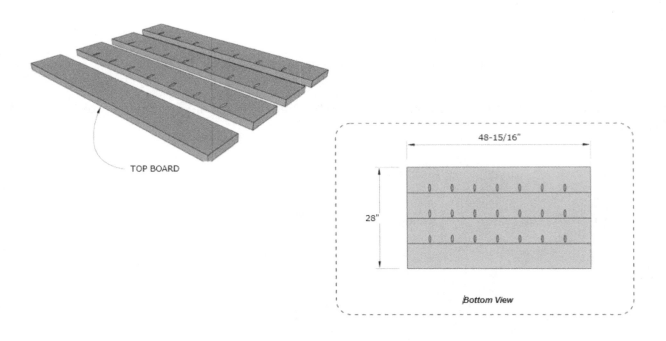

TOP BOARD

48-15/16"

28"

Bottom View

Assemble the tabletop.

Install the top of slides onto the tabletop. Then attach to the base of the table.

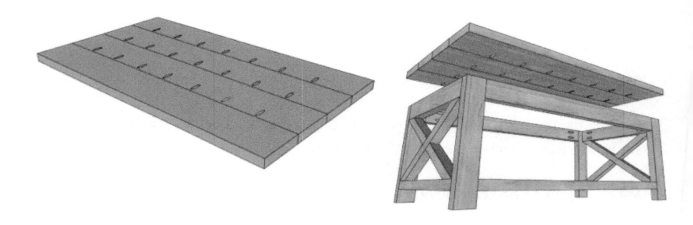

Bottom shelf:

Turn the table on its side. Attach bottom shelf boards using pre-drilled holes in the shelf for support. Use 1 1/4¨screws.

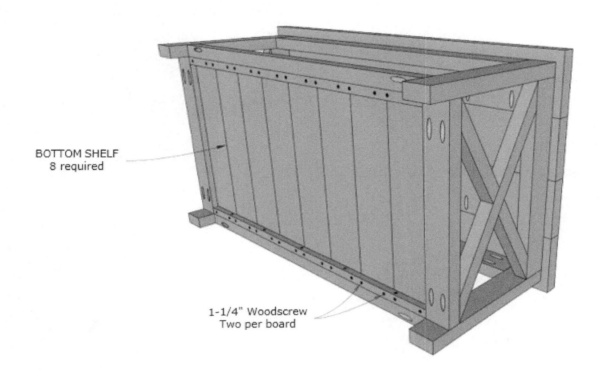

BOTTOM SHELF
8 required

1-1/4" Woodscrew
Two per board

BIRD HOUSE

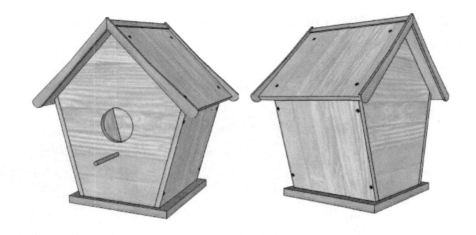

EXPLODED VIEW – EACH PIECE IDENTIFIED

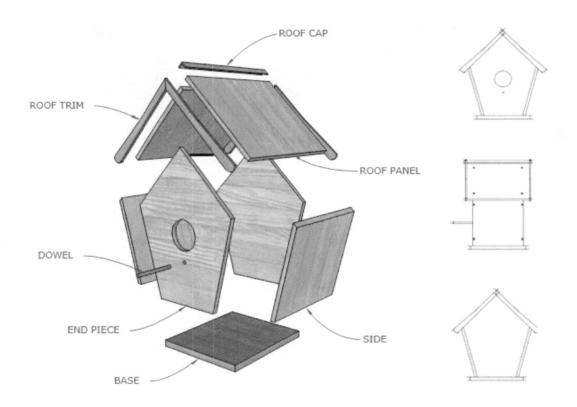

ROOF CAP

ROOF TRIM

ROOF PANEL

DOWEL

END PIECE

SIDE

BASE

Material list:

Part	Description	Quantity	Length	Width	Thickness	Material
A	BASE	1	11 1/2"	11"	3/4"	1x Wood
B	SIDE	2	11"	10 1/2"	1/2"	1/2 Plywood
C	END PIECE	2	17 1/2"	13 11/16"	1/2"	1/2 Plywood
D	ROOF PANEL	1	13"	11"	1/2"	1/2 Plywood
E	ROOF PANEL	1	13"	11 1/2"	1/2"	1/2 Plywood
F	ROOF TRIM	4	12 3/8"	1 1/8"	1/4"	1/4 Plywood
G	ROOF CAP	1	13"	3/4"	3/4"	1x Wood
H	DOWEL	1	4"	3/8"	3/8"	

Base & Sides:

Make a 3/4"- thick base (A), glue up a 12"- square blank.

Side (B) and end pieces (C) are cut from 1/2"-thick exterior plywood. See the drawing below.

Center the pieces and screw them in place.

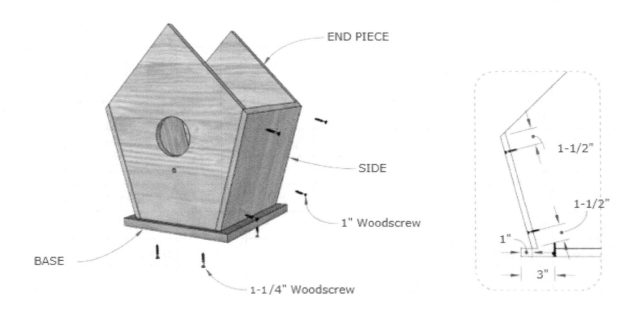

END PIECE

SIDE

1" Woodscrew

BASE

1-1/4" Woodscrew

1-1/2"

1-1/2"

1"

3"

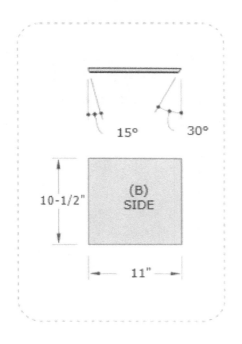

15°   30°

10-1/2"

(B)
SIDE

11"

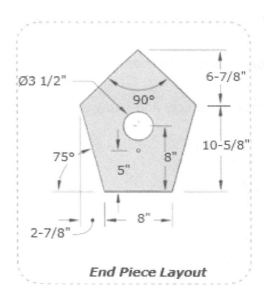

Ø3 1/2"

90°

6-7/8"

75°

8"

10-5/8"

5"

8"

2-7/8"

End Piece Layout

Roof panels:

Center the roof panels (E) and (D) and screw them in place.

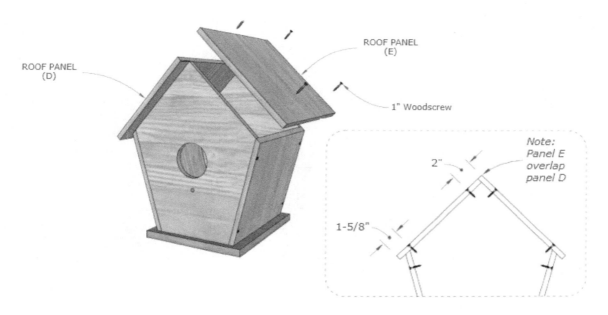

Trim:

Install roof trim (F) first, then cut roof cap (G) to fit between them. Use glue and 1" nails.

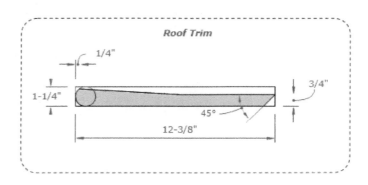

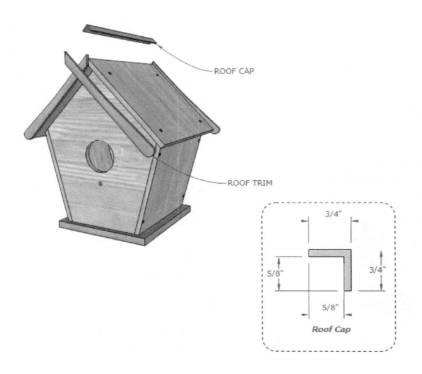

ROOF CAP

ROOF TRIM

3/4"

5/8"   3/4"

5/8"

Roof Cap

Dowel:

The last piece to add to the bird house is the 3/8" dowel. Glue and insert inside the lower hole.

Made in the USA
Las Vegas, NV
17 December 2023

83028814R00079